Carol Field Dahlstrom

Christmas together

Craft · Share · Bake · Decorate · Give · Celebrate

Carol Field Dahlstrom, Inc.
Brave Ink Press
Ankeny, Iowa

Author and Editor
Carol Field Dahlstrom

Book Design
Lyne Neymeyer

Photography
Pete Krumhardt, Dean Tanner— Primary Image, Lyne Neymeyer Photo/Design
Copy Editing: Jill Philby, Janet Figg
Proofreading: Jan Temeyer, Elizabeth Dahlstrom
Food Artist: Jennifer Peterson
Exclusive Art: Susan Cornelison, Allison May
Props and Location: Roger Dahlstrom
Technical Assistant: Judy Bailey
How-to Illustrations: Kristen Krumhardt
Recipe Development and Testing: Ardith Field, Barbara Hoover, Elizabeth Dahlstrom

**Special thanks to these people for helping to make some
of the items in the book:** Kristin Detrick, Ardith Field, Barbara Hoover, Janet Petersma,
Jennifer Peterson, Ann E. Smith, Jan Temeyer

ISBN 0-9679764-8-0
Library of Congress Control Number: 2005902215
Copyright © Carol Field Dahlstrom, Inc. 2005

Separations: Scan Graphics, Des Moines, Iowa
Printed in the United States of America
First Edition

While all of the information has been checked and tested, human error can occur.
Carol Field Dahlstrom, Inc. and Brave Ink Press cannot be held responsible for any loss or injury
associated with the making of any project or information in this book.

Carol Field Dahlstrom, Inc. and Brave Ink Press strive to provide high quality products and information
that will make your life happier and more beautiful. Please write or e-mail us with your comments,
questions, and suggestions or to inquire about purchasing books at braveink@aol.com or
Brave Ink Press, P.O. Box 663, Ankeny, Iowa 50021.

Visit us at www.braveink.com to see upcoming books from Brave Ink Press or to purchase books.
The "I can do that!" books™

Time Together

 There is never enough time—especially at Christmastime. We imagine holding hands and taking walks in the wintry snow or giving a hug to a special friend that we haven't seen for years. We think about cuddling up with a cup of hot cocoa and reading our Christmas cards as holiday music is playing. We dream about the quiet nights around the Christmas tree with the lights twinkling as we sit with our friends and family laughing and telling stories of Christmases past.

But somehow things don't always work out that way. We are tired after shopping. We feel pressured to make every corner of the house perfect for the holidays. Sometimes we forget what Christmas is all about as we get lost in the convincing ads and gotta-haves.

We know you want to make your time together really count. So in this book we've shared ideas for decorating, crafting, gift giving, cooking and enjoying the season that are simple yet beautiful. Find time to create your Christmas dreams together—the process of making things together is the most fun of all. And many of the projects and ideas in this book can be made in just a few minutes, leaving you more time together to celebrate the holiday.

So this year hold hands a little longer, hug a little tighter, laugh a little more often, and enjoy your Christmas Together.

Carol Field Dahlstrom

Contents

Welcome them Home

The snow is falling, the candles are lit, the stockings are hung, and hearts are filled with excitement as you all anticipate a wonderful Christmas homecoming. Get ready for the holiday magic with clever ideas to welcome them home.

Christmas Homecoming

Welcome them home by decorating your entry with the beloved colors of Christmas. To make it look even sweeter, add a little Christmas candy and offer a wrapped gift to everyone that comes to call.

 Your guests will feel the holiday spirit when they are welcomed by traditional colors of the season. Give your pretty holiday wreath a sweet twist by adding a little peppermint candy. Add the candy as we did in our **Christmas Twist Wreath** by wiring flat peppermints onto a purchased berry wreath. Attach a big red bow with long streamers to finish the look. Instructions for making the wreath are on page 22. Turn the page for more Christmas Homecoming ideas.

To finish your colorful Christmas entry, set some **Candy Luminarias** on the doorstep to light the way. Fill a canning jar with candies and tie a ribbon around the jar that spells out your holiday sentiments. Instructions for making the luminarias are on page 22.

Decorate a little tree with gifts for everyone who comes to your door. Purchase little boxes to wrap and then choose items that fit into the boxes that will make your guests feel the holiday spirit. Pieces of wrapped candy, inexpensive jewelry, tickets to holiday events, a tiny Santa figurine, pretty paper clips, or a votive candle are just a few ideas to put in your Christmas boxes. Set the tree on a little chair or bench to greet your holiday visitors.

Birdie Trims

Decorate the trees on the outside of your holiday home to greet visitors of all kinds. These clever **Birdie Trims** are made of ice and hold tasty surprises for your feathered friends. Instructions for making the icy ornaments are on page 23.

Winter Wonderland

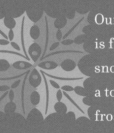

CREATE YOUR OWN HOLIDAY SNOW FUN
BY MAKING A FRONT-DOOR GREETING
SURE TO BRING WINTER SMILES.

Our **Snowball Envelope**
is filled with faux
snowballs, icy picks, and
a touch of greenery. The
frosty railing and icy
trees use the same faux snowballs for their
winter look. The **Winter White
Luminarias** are quick to make using rice,
votive candles, and soft white ribbon.
Instructions for all of the projects are on
pages 24-25.

13

Spelled-Out Greetings

SPELL IT OUT FOR THEM AS THEY COME TO CALL AND THEY'LL FEEL ALL THE MORE WELCOME.

 Metal words available at scrapbook and craft stores make clever **Spelled-Out Greetings** that are as much fun to make as they are to read. Just add beads and wire to create ornaments or a doorknob greeting. For instructions see page 26.

Pretty Holiday Welcome

COMBINE THE ELEGANCE AND TRADITION OF THE WELCOMING
PINEAPPLE AND THE EXOTIC COLORS OF NATURAL PEACOCK
FEATHERS TO MAKE YOUR HOLIDAY ENTRANCE SING WITH THE
BEAUTY OF THE SEASON.

 Begin by creating a **Pineapple Door Swag**, opposite and above, using a pineapple as the center of the piece. Add colorful peacock feathers and frosted greens to surround the pineapple and finish it with a lime-green bow.

Make a **Pineapple Luminaria**, opposite and below, by carving candle holders into the fruit and adding green votive candles to finish the look.

Turn simple evergreen trees into part of your holiday entrance theme by decorating them with peacock feathers, bunches of sugared acrylic grapes, and bows in the colors of the theme. Arrange peacock feathers and long cut greens in a ceramic pot to finish the pretty holiday entrance.

Instructions for making the projects are on page 27.

Home-Sweetest-Home Sugar Cookies

THEY'LL LOVE THE LOOK AND KNOW THEY'RE HOME WHEN THEY SEE THESE CLEVER AND OH-SO-TASTY COOKIES THAT YOU MADE JUST FOR THEM.

The secret to making these delightful **Home-Sweetest-Home Sugar Cookies** is to layer simple cookie squares and triangles and then to decorate them like your holiday home or the home of your sugar plum dreams. Serve the cookies as they are, or hang them on your Christmas tree to create a cookie village. The recipe and tips for making these sweet cookies are on pages 28-29.

18

Goodie Goodie Fireplace

COLORFUL COOKIE STOCKINGS
HANG FROM A WARM AND TOASTY
PEANUT STONE FIREPLACE.

Use your favorite
Christmas treats
to create a
**Goodie Goodie
Fireplace** to
warm their hearts. The structure of
the cozy piece is created using flat
gingerbread shapes, and the layers
of goodies are peanuts held in place
with sweet white icing.

Pretty cookie stockings all
covered with polka-dots hang on
the mantel to make the piece a real
holiday showpiece. For recipes and
instructions to make the fireplace,
see pages 30-31.

Christmas Twist Wreath

Shown on pages 8-9

What you need

- Purchased 18-inch red berry wreath
- 24 gauge wire; wire cutters
- Sprig of evergreen— real or artificial
- Flat peppermint candies
- 1½ yards of 2-inch-wide red satin ribbon trimmed with gold
- 2 yards of 1-inch-wide red satin ribbon trimmed with gold

What you do

If the purchased wreath doesn't have a loop for hanging, make a loop using the wire and attach at the back. Place the evergreen on the wreath and wire in place. Unwrap the peppermints and wrap the wire around them like an X, leaving wire in the back for attaching to the wreath. Wire the candies onto the wreath where desired. Cut the 1-inch-wide ribbon into 24-inch length streamers. Fold the pieces in half and wire in the middle at the top of the wreath. Make a bow using the wide ribbon and wire it on top of the small ribbon streamers. For tips on bow-making, see page 156.

Candy Luminarias

Shown on pages 8, 10

What you need

- Wide mouth, pint-sized fruit jars
- Flat peppermint candies
- Red votive candles
- Conversation holiday ribbons

What you do

Be sure the fruit jars are clean and dry. Unwrap the candies and set aside. Place the votive in the center bottom of the jar. Drop the candies around the candle until the jar is about ½ full. Tie the ribbon around the top of the jar. Trim the ribbon ends. *Never leave a burning candle unattended.*

Birdie Trims

Shown on page 11

What you need

- **Gelatin molds or other holiday-shaped mold**
- **Natural string**
- **Bird seed**
- **Cranberries or other berries**
- **Orange peels**
- **Water**
- **Freezer or cold outdoor temperatures**

What you do

Cut the natural string into 8-inch pieces. Loop the string and lay the cut ends over the edge into the inside of each mold or muffin cup. See photo A. You can make more than one bird ornament at a time. Arrange the bird treats in the bottom of the mold. Use any food items that are safe for the birds and attract birds in your geographical area.

Fill the molds with water and freeze in the freezer or set outside in below freezing temperatures to freeze. Rearrange the string if needed so it freezes in the mold but still makes a loop. After the water has turned to ice, remove from the mold and hang on the tree outside.

Here's a Crafting Secret

YOU CAN MAKE ALL KINDS OF ICY PROJECTS FOR CHRISTMAS. MAKE AN ICE WREATH BY FREEZING PRETTY CRANBERRIES, RASPBERRIES, BLUEBERRIES AND FRESH ROSEMARY WITH WATER IN A BUNDT CAKE PAN. PLACE IN THE FREEZER OR OUTSIDE TO FREEZE AND THEN HANG OUTSIDE ON COLD WINTER DAYS.

Winter Wonderland
Snowball Envelope
Shown on pages 12—13

What you need

- **Purchased tin "envelope style" door decoration (available at crafts stores)**
- **White spray paint**
- **2- or 3-inch-wide white Styrofoam balls**
- **Bamboo skewer**
- **Flat piece of Styrofoam**
- **Table knife**
- **Gesso**
- **White glitter**
- **Greens—real or artificial**
- **Icy picks (available in the floral department at crafts stores)**
- **1 ½-inch-wide sheer white wire-edge ribbon**
- **Fine wire**

What you do

In a well-ventilated area, spray paint the door decoration white. Allow to dry. Set aside.

To make the "snowballs", use the table knife to layer the gesso on the ball. See photo A, below. Layer it thick enough to resemble snow. While it is still wet, sprinkle with glitter. Poke one end of the skewer into the ball and the other end into the flat piece of Styrofoam to secure it until it is dry. See photo B, below.

Fill the spray-painted envelope decoration with greens, icy picks, and the snowballs. Make a bow using the white ribbon. See page 156 for tips on tying bows. Wire the bow to the front of the painted envelope. Hang on door.

A

B

Winter White Luminarias

Shown on pages 12—13

What you need

- Desired size canning jar
- Paper doily
- Scissors
- Masking tape
- White spray paint
- White rice
- White votive candle
- White ribbon for bow

What you do

Be sure the canning jar is clean and dry. Cut a section of the doily and lay it on the jar, overlapping the ends. Secure with tape. See photo at left.

In a well-ventilated area, spray paint the jar lightly with the white paint only over the doily. Let dry and remove the doily.

Place the white votive candle in the bottom of the jar and pour rice around the candle. Tie a bow at the top of the jar. *Never leave a burning candle unattended.*

Here's a Crafting Secret

TO MAKE IT EASIER TO POUR THE RICE INTO THE JAR, USE A SMALL PURCHASED FUNNEL OR MAKE ONE YOURSELF USING A PIECE OF CARDSTOCK-WEIGHT PAPER. TO MAKE A PAPER FUNNEL, CUT A 10-INCH CIRCLE FROM THE PAPER AND THEN CUT A SLIT UP TO THE CENTER FROM ONE SIDE. CUT A $\frac{1}{4}$-INCH PIE WEDGE FROM THE CIRCLE. MAKE THE CIRCLE INTO A CONE AND CUT $\frac{1}{2}$-INCH TIP FROM THE END. TAPE OR STAPLE THE PAPER FUNNEL TOGETHER AND USE IT TO FILL THE LUMINARIAS.

Spelled-Out Greetings

Shown on pages 14–15

What you need

• **Purchased word greetings (available at scrapbook and art stores, or see Sources, page 157)**

• **Small awl or hammer and small nail**

• **24-gauge wire**

• **Beads in colors that you like**

What you do
For the ornaments,
choose the word that you wish. Use the awl or small nail and hammer to make small holes at the top of each end of the word. Measure a piece of wire about 10 inches long. Temporarily loop one end of the wire to keep the beads from falling off. Plan the bead arrangement that you like and thread the beads onto the wire. Place the end of the wire through one of the holes and twist to secure. Unloop the other wire and place through the other hole. Twist to secure. Hang on the tree.

For the door decoration, choose the words that you wish. Lay them out to be sure they can be stacked on top of each other and have a space for making the holes. Use the awl or small nail and hammer to make small holes at the top and bottom at the ends of the words. Measure the wire to fit between the words, leaving enough to loop through the holes and secure. Arrange the beads and finish the decoration as for the ornaments.

Here's a Crafting Secret

WHEN MAKING HOLES IN CRAFTING METAL USING A HAMMER AND SMALL NAIL OR AN AWL, PLACE A PIECE OF WOOD OR OLD CUTTING BOARD UNDER THE METAL. THE HOLE IN THE METAL WILL BE CLEANER AND YOUR WORK TABLE WILL STAY IN GOOD SHAPE.

Pretty Holiday Welcome
Pineapple Door Swag
Shown on pages 16—17

What you need

- Purchased evergreen swag
- Purchased fan-type stick wreath form
- 20-gauge wire; wire cutters
- Pineapple
- Sharp knife
- Dried florals on sticks as desired
- Peacock feathers
- Hot glue gun and hot glue sticks
- 3 yards of 2-inch-wide lime-green ribbon

What you do

Wire the evergreen swag to the bottom of the fan-type form creating the triangular shape swag. Add a loop of wire on the back at the top for hanging. Cut the pineapple in half the long way. Wire it to the center of the swag by wrapping the wire around the pineapple stem and body. Twist in the back to secure. Hot glue the floral sticks and peacock feathers to the swag hiding the stems behind the pineapple when possible. Pull the greenery around to hide any other gluing. Tie a bow and wire to the swag. For hints on bow-making, see page 156.

Pineapple Luminaria
Shown on pages 16—17

What you need

- Pineapple
- Sharp knife
- Pencil
- Green votive candles

What you do

Choose a pineapple that is slightly flat on one side or slice off one side slightly so the pineapple will lay horizontally.

Mark three holes on the top of the pineapple and use the sharp knife to make holes where marked. Place the votives in the holes. *Note:* If you are using this outside and wind is a problem, place the votives in glass holders before inserting into the pineapple. *Never leave a burning candle unattended.*

Home-Sweet-Home Sugar Cookies

Shown on pages 18–19

What you need

- 3 cups all-purpose flour
- 1 teaspoon baking powder
- ¼ teaspoon salt
- 1 cup butter, softened
- 1 cup sugar
- 1 egg
- 2 teaspoons vanilla
- 3 tablespoons milk
- 1 recipe Meringue Icing
- Paste food coloring (pink, leaf green, sky blue, golden yellow) available at discount and craft stores
- Disposable decorating bag with coupler and small round and/or star tips, available at discount and crafts stores
- Pastel candy decorations and pastel decorating sugars See Sources, page 157

What you do

In a large bowl stir together flour, baking powder and salt. In another bowl beat butter with an electric mixer. Beat in sugar until well combined and fluffy. Beat in egg until well combined. Beat in vanilla and milk. Gradually beat in flour mixture, using a spoon if too thick for mixer.

Divide dough into two portions. Wrap in plastic wrap and chill several hours or until easy to handle.

Roll out chilled dough on a lightly floured surface to about ¼ to ⅛ inch thick.

To make house shapes, cut out a few cookies using assorted square cookie cutters or cut squares in 1 to 3 inch square shapes. Cut some of the squares in half forming triangles to create roof pieces. Arrange the cookies on the baking sheet, overlapping as desired to create different house shapes. See photo A, opposite.

If desired, make a hole for hanging using the end of a straw to poke a hole at the top of the cookie. Bake in a 375 degree oven for 8 to 10 minutes or until edges just begin to brown.

Let cool on cookie sheet for 2 minutes. Remove to a wire rack to cool completely.

Meringue Icing: In a medium bowl beat together 3 tablespoons meringue powder, ½ teaspoon cream of tartar, 1 teaspoon clear vanilla, and ½ cup warm water with an electric mixer. Beat in 4½ cups sifted powdered sugar on low speed until combined. Beat on high speed for about 5 minutes or until thickened and white. For decorating techniques shown, thin the icing by gradually adding water until icing is a flowing consistency, like pancake batter.
Makes about 3 cups.

Decorators tip: When working with many different icing colors over an extended period of time, it is helpful to place the small batches of tinted icing in very small disposable round containers with lids. The icings can be stored overnight in refrigerator. Stir icings before using again to restore consistency.

For each color to be tinted, place about ½ cup Meringue Icing in a small bowl. Keep remaining icing covered when not using. Tint icing desired colors with a small amount of food coloring.

Gradually stir in a little water, ½ teaspoon at a time, until icing is thin enough to paint on cookies.

Use a clean artist's brush to paint a base coat of desired icing color onto cookie houses. Let dry about an hour. Meanwhile, fit a decorating bag with a coupler and small round or star tip.

Fill bag with some remaining stiff white icing. Pipe house details like windows, doors, holiday decorations, and snow onto cookies. While piped icing is still wet, you may sprinkle with pastel sugars or other candy decorations. Let decorated cookies dry for 1 to 2 hours.

A

Goodie Goodie Fireplace

Shown on pages 20—21

What you need

- 5½ cups all-purpose flour
- 2 teaspoons ground ginger
- 2 teaspoons ground cinnamon
- ½ teaspoon ground cloves
- ¾ teaspoon baking soda
- ¼ teaspoon baking powder
- 1 cup butter, softened
- 1 cup packed dark brown sugar
- 1 cup light molasses
- 2 eggs
- Meringue Icing (see page 29)
- 3 cups honey-roasted peanuts
- Few pretzel logs
- Fruit Roll-Ups, red and yellow
- Few gumdrops
- Four fresh rosemary sprigs
- Ribbon, ⅛ inch wide
- Stocking shaped cookie cutters, see Sources, page 157

fireplace top and bottom—cut 2

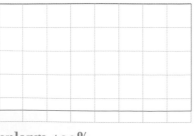

enlarge 400%

What you do

In a large bowl stir together flour, ginger, cinnamon, cloves, baking soda, and baking powder. In another bowl beat butter with an electric mixer. Beat in brown sugar until fluffy. Beat in molasses and eggs until well combined. Gradually beat in flour mixture. Use a wooden spoon if dough is too thick for mixer. Divide dough in fourths. Wrap dough in plastic wrap and chill several hours or until easy to handle.

Cutting and Baking

Enlarge patterns below, on to clean paper and cut out. Use a floured rolling pin to roll one portion of dough at a time on a 15x12-inch piece of parchment paper till ⅛ to ¼-inch thick. Place patterns 1 inch apart on dough; cut around patterns with a sharp knife. Remove excess dough. Place parchment on a large baking sheet. Bake cookie pieces in a 375 degree oven for 10 to 12 minutes or till edges are browned. While pieces are still very warm, place patterns on cookies and trim excess. Return pieces to oven for about 2 minutes or till firm in center. Remove the parchment from baking sheet and cool on a wire rack. Remove cookie pieces from parchment when cool. Cut stocking cookies using stocking cookie cutter. Make hole in top using a straw if necessary. Bake and set aside.

Constructing the Fireplace Structure

Fit a decorating bag with coupler and a medium-sized (⅛ inch opening) round tip. Fill with some Meringue Icing. If decorating tip becomes clogged with dry icing, wipe with a damp cloth. Prepared icing may be stored overnight in the refrigerator. To use after storing, beat with an electric mixer till very stiff. Have glass tumblers or coffee mugs handy to hold pieces in place while assembling.

On a piece of parchment paper, set out bottom, front, back, and sides of fireplace. Attach back of fireplace to bottom using a line of icing where pieces touch. (See photo A.) Hold in place with tumblers or mugs. Attach sides, front, and top in same manner. When icing is set, (about an hour) remove all supports. Check to make sure mantle piece fits around fireplace. Carefully trim with a serrated knife if necessary. Locate items to support the mantle at desired height. Attach mantle to fireplace with more piped icing and support until dry (1 to 2 hours).

Decorating Stockings and Fireplace

Gradually add some water to thin icing to a flowing consistency, like pancake batter. Divide icing into 4 portions. With toothpicks, add desired color of paste food coloring to each portion. Keep icing covered to prevent drying. Use a clean artist's brush to paint base coat of icing on one cookie. While icing is still wet, add a second color making stripes or polka dots by drizzling or painting with brush. Let iced cookies dry overnight.

To cover fireplace with "stones", spread stiff icing onto one small area of fireplace. Press peanuts into the icing. Continue spreading icing and adding peanuts until fireplace is covered. Back of fireplace is optional and will take extra icing and peanuts. To make four gumdrop pots for hanging stockings, poke a small hole in wide end of gumdrops with a skewer. Use some stiff white icing to attach pots, wide end up, to mantle. Let icing dry well before hanging any stockings.

For logs, use broken pretzels held together with icing. To make a flame, sandwich together two pieces of fruit roll-ups. Cut out a 4x2-inch rectangle. Cut out pointed notches along top edge. Gather bottom edge and attach to log pile with some icing. Thread ribbon through dried, iced stockings. Tie a loop and hang from set pots. For rosemary topiaries, trim a sprig of rosemary into a pine tree shape and insert the stem into a gumdrop pot.

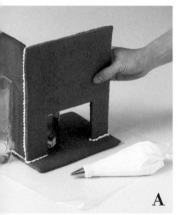
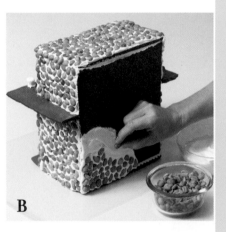

A B

**fireplace front and back—
cut 1 front and one back**

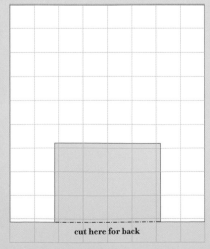

cut here for back

fireplace sides—cut 2

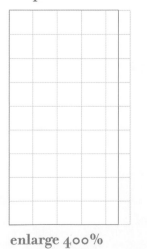

fireplace mantle—cut 1

enlarge 400%   enlarge 400%   enlarge 400%   31

Cuddle Up with Christmas Comforts

The holiday lights are twinkling and the air is cold and crisp—Christmas is near. Whether you are out caroling, sledding, ice skating, or just taking a walk, there is nothing more cozy than coming in from the cold to be greeted by a smile, hot cocoa, and a freshly baked treat. Try your hand at making the wintery chill disappear by creating some goodies for someone you love.

Holiday Mitten Bread

 They'll all be smiling when they see the bread plate filled with warm and tasty **Holiday Mitten Bread**. Use your favorite bread dough recipe or use frozen bread dough to create this fun and yummy treat. The recipe is on page 44.

Hearty Wild Rice Soup

Steamy and hot and filled with all kinds of healthy goodness, **Hearty Wild-Rice Soup** is quick to make and oh-so-delicious. Serve it with a favorite bread for a special holiday treat. The recipe is on page 44.

Lemon Poppy Seed Muffins

Lemon Poppy Seed Muffins are sure to be a hit any time of year, but at the holidays they taste even better. Top them off with a powdered sugar glaze and sprinkle with coarse white sugar. The recipe is on page 45.

White Chocolate Cocoa

 Heavenly and creamy, our must-have **White Chocolate Cocoa** seems almost too good to be true. The smooth and creamy texture is sweetened with white chocolate chips and some tiny marshmallows. Stir up a big batch to have on hand to serve the crowd after Christmas caroling. The recipe is on page 45.

Make it a Gift

Anyone would love to get a little jar of white chocolate cocoa mix for Christmas. Little milk bottles can be found at flea markets or use any little glass jar. Just layer the mix, add a piece of colored paper on top, and tie on a tag with instructions for making this sweet treat.

Christmas Citrus Tea

 **Christmas Citrus Tea** will be the holiday choice for everyone who stops by to wish you the best. Choose a favorite tea and add sweet strips of candied orange peel that you make yourself. The flavors combine to make this hot drink one that they will ask for year after year. The recipe for making the tea and orange peel is on page 47.

Make it a Gift

Choose a pretty little tea cup and fill it with candied orange peel. Use a colorful holiday ribbon to tie on a favorite tea bag and some christmas ornaments and you've just made a lovely gift for any tea lover.

Swedish Glögg

As warm and delicious as it is beautiful, **Swedish Glögg** is sure to become a family tradition. The spices and warm wine combine to make an unmistakably wonderful combination. Serve with holiday crackers or cookies. The recipe is on page 46.

Make it a Gift

MAKE A GIFT OF WINE EVEN MORE APPEALING BY TYING ALL THE INGREDIENTS NEEDED TO MAKE THE SWEDISH GLÖGG TO THE BOTTLE WITH A PRETTY RIBBON AND A COLORFUL ORNAMENT. MAKE YOUR OWN "HOW-TO-MAKE-IT" CARD OR USE THE PREPRINTED GIFT CARD ON PAGE 46.

Orange Cranberry Muffins

Sweet oranges and tart cranberries combine to make a muffin that is warm, delicious, and so inviting. Cuddle up with your favorite book, a Christmas carol, and a warm **Orange Cranberry Muffin** to make a holiday evening complete. The recipe is on page 47.

Hot Spiced Cider

 Bring them in from the cold with a simple holiday favorite—**Hot Spiced Cider**. Have all the ingredients on hand for anytime the weather is cold and snowy outside so you can warm their hearts and tummies in no time. The recipe is on page 48.

Make it a Gift

 FOR A SPECIAL GIFT, FILL A QUART CANNING JAR WITH CIDER AND PUT ALL OF THE OTHER INGREDIENTS IN A LITTLE PIECE OF CHEESECLOTH TO SPICE UP THE PRESENTATION. ADD A GIFT TAG WITH DIRECTIONS FOR MAKING THE SWEET DRINK. COMPLETE INSTRUCTIONS FOR MAKING THE GIFT PRESENTATION ARE ON PAGE 48. MAKE YOUR OWN "HOW-TO-MAKE-IT" CARD OR USE THE PREPRINTED GIFT CARD ON PAGE 48.

41

Holiday Cocoa Mix

Traditional hot cocoa gets easier when you make your own mix and have it on hand for any winter activity—sledding, caroling, or making angels in the snow. The recipe is on page 49.

Make it a Gift

GIVE THIS YUMMY COCOA MIX AS A GIFT BY LAYERING THE MIX IN A DISPOSABLE CAKE DECORATING BAG (AVAILABLE AT CRAFT, DISCOUNT, AND KITCHEN STORES). MAKE YOUR OWN "HOW-TO-MAKE-IT" CARD OR USE THE PRETTY PREPRINTED GIFT CARD ON PAGE 49.

Rich Christmas Coffee Mix

 You won't need to stand in line to get a cup of rich coffee to celebrate the season. This easy-to-make mix is perfect to have on hand for a cup of coffee while you're wrapping those packages late at night. Make plenty of the mix and give away for gifts—your friends will love you for it! The recipe is on page 49.

Make it a Gift

A JAR OF THIS DELICIOUS COFFEE MIX WILL BE A FAVORITE GIFT FOR THE COFFEE LOVER ON YOUR CHRISTMAS LIST. FILL A JAR WITH THE MIX AND ADD A RIBBON AND INSTRUCTIONS FOR MAKING INDIVIDUAL SERVINGS OF THE COFFEE. FOR INSTRUCTIONS AND A PRINTED GIFT CARD, SEE PAGE 49.

Holiday Mitten Bread

Shown on page 34

What you need

- Purchased frozen bread dough (one loaf makes about 4 large mittens)
- One egg yolk
- 1 tablespoon water
- Food coloring
- Small (clean and new) paint brush

What you do

Allow the frozen bread loaf to thaw but not rise. Cut the loaf into four pieces. Divide each of those pieces into one large and two small pieces. Roll one of the little pieces into a quarter-size ball for the thumb. Flatten the other little piece into a strip for the cuff. See photo at left. Form the big ball into a mitten shape. Use your hands or rolling pin to flatten the mitten. Add the "thumb" by attaching the little ball to the big ball and working it into the side with a table knife. Add the cuff and then use a sharp knife to make indentations on the cuff of the mitten.

Add the water to the egg yolk and mix well. Add desired colors of food coloring. Paint the mitten designs on the bread. Allow the bread to rise for about ½ hour. Bake as instructed on the frozen bread package.

Hearty Wild Rice Soup

Shown on page 35

What you need

- 6 tablespoons butter
- 2 tablespoons chopped green onions
- ¼ cup shredded carrots
- ¼ cup flour
- 4 cups chicken broth
- 2 cups cooked and drained wild rice
- ⅔ cup sliced fresh mushrooms
- 1 cup half and half
- Salt and pepper

What you do

Melt the butter in a heavy saucepan. Cook the green onions and carrots in the hot butter. Add the flour and mix well. Pour in the chicken broth and bring to a boil. Boil one minute. Add the wild rice, mushrooms and half and half. Add salt and pepper to taste. Heat but do not boil. Serve immediately. Makes 6 servings.

Lemon Poppy Seed Muffins

Shown on page 36

What you need

- 2 eggs
- 1 cup whole milk
- ¼ cup canola oil
- 2 tablespoons poppy seeds
- ⅓ cup sugar
- 3 teaspoons baking powder
- ½ teaspoon salt
- 1 tablespoon grated lemon rind
- 2¼ cups all-purpose flour

Lemon Powdered Sugar Glaze

- 3 tablespoons lemon juice
- 1 cup powdered sugar
- Coarse white sugar

What you do

Preheat oven to 400 degrees. Grease bottoms of medium-sized muffin pan. Beat eggs and milk and stir in oil. Mix flour and poppy seeds together and add to mixture. Stir in all other ingredients and mix until just blended. Do not overmix. Batter should be lumpy.

Fill muffin cups ¾ full. Bake for about 15 minutes or until golden brown. Makes 12 muffins.
To make glaze, stir together the lemon juice and powdered sugar until smooth. Drizzle over the top of each muffin and sprinkle with coarse white sugar.

White Chocolate Cocoa

Shown on page 37

What you need

- 2 cups non fat dry milk
- 2 cups sifted powdered sugar
- 2 cups powdered non dairy creamer
- ½ cup white chocolate chips
- Miniature marshmallows

What you do

In a bowl combine dry milk, sugar, and creamer. Add white chocolate chips. Store in tightly covered container. For two servings, measure ⅔ cup mix and 1½ cups very hot water. Stir until well blended or until most of chips have melted. Divide between two mugs and add a few marshmallows. Makes about 18 servings.

Swedish Glögg

Shown on page 39

What you need

- Few pieces Candied Orange Peel, see recipe, page 47, or use purchased orange peel
- 8 inches stick cinnamon
- 6 whole cloves
- 2 cardamom pods, opened
- ½ cup mixed golden raisins and cherries
- ¼ cup slivered almonds
- Cheesecloth, kitchen string, and small plastic bags
- 1 bottle red wine
- ⅓ cup sugar

What you do

For spice bag, place orange peel, cinnamon, cloves, and cardamom in center of a double-thick, 6-inch square of cotton cheesecloth. Bring up corners and tie tightly with kitchen string. (For gift giving, place spice bag in a plastic bag along with raisins, almonds, and orange peel. Seal bag.)

In a large saucepan combine wine, spice bag, raisins, almonds, and candied orange peel. Add ⅓ cup sugar.

Heat mixture to simmering. Simmer uncovered for 10 minutes. Do not boil. Remove spice bag and discard. To serve, fill each cup with a few raisins, almonds, peel, and a ladle-full of wine mixture.

To give as a gift, give plastic bag along with a bottle of wine and the directions for preparing.

Merry Christmas to:

In a large saucepan combine wine, spice bag, raisins, almonds, and candied orange peel. Add ⅓ cup sugar. Heat mixture to simmering. Simmer uncovered for 10 minutes. Do not boil. Remove spice bag and discard.
To serve, fill each cup with a few raisins, almonds, peel, and a ladle-full of the wine mixture. Enjoy!

From,

Christmas Citrus Tea

Shown on page 38

What you need

- Favorite tea bag
- Candied Orange Peel

Candied Orange Peel

- 4 unblemished navel oranges
- 3 cups sugar
- ½ cup water
- ⅓ cup corn syrup
- Sugar

What you do

Wash oranges and cut each into 6 wedges. Scrape away the pulp leaving the peel with the white membrane attached. Place peels into saucepan, cover with cold water, and bring to a boil. Boil 1 minute; drain off water. Repeat three more times. Remove peels from saucepan and set aside. Add sugar, water and corn syrup to pan. Bring to boil over medium-high heat, stirring to dissolve sugar. Meanwhile cut peels into ¼-inch wide strips. When sugar is dissolved, add the peels and turn heat down to medium. Boil for 25 to 30 minutes or until most of the syrup is absorbed and the peels are glossy. Place on cooling rack. When cool enough to handle, toss a few strips at a time in a bowl filled with sugar. Return strips to rack to dry for 2 to 3 hours. Store in airtight container in refrigerator for up to 6 months. Prepare tea. Add orange peel.

Orange Cranberry Muffins

Shown on page 40

What you need

- 2 eggs
- 1½ cups buttermilk
- ⅓ cup salad oil
- 2½ cups all-purpose flour
- ⅓ cup sugar
- 2 teaspoons baking powder
- ½ teaspoon baking soda
- ½ teaspoon salt
- 1 tablespoon grated orange rind
- ¾ cup dried cranberries

Topping

- 3 tablespoons yellow decorator sugar
- 1 teaspoon ground cinnamon

What you do

Preheat oven to 400 degrees. Grease bottoms of medium-sized muffin cup pan. Beat eggs and milk and stir in oil. Stir in all other ingredients and mix until just blended. Batter should be lumpy. Do not overmix. Fill muffin cups ¾ full. Mix sugar and cinnamon together and sprinkle a little of the mixture on top of each muffin. Bake for about 15 minutes or until golden brown. Makes 12 muffins.

Hot Spiced Cider

Shown on page 41

What you need

- **3 inches stick cinnamon**
- **½ teaspoon whole allspice**
- **½ teaspoon whole cloves**
- **1 star anise**
- **Few pieces Candied Orange Peel (from recipe, page 47, or use purchased)**
- **Cheesecloth and kitchen string**
- **1 quart apple juice or apple cider**
- **3 tablespoons brown sugar**

What you do

Create a spice bag of mulling spices to put in the cider while it heats. To make the spice bag, place stick cinnamon (broken into pieces), allspice, cloves, anise, and orange peel in center of a double-thick, 6-inch square of cotton cheesecloth. Bring up corners and tie tightly with some kitchen string.

In a large saucepan or crockery cooker, combine apple juice, brown sugar, and the spice bag. Simmer for 10 minutes in saucepan or up to 2 hours in small crockery cooker. Remove spice bag before serving the cider.

To give as a gift:

FILL A QUART-SIZE JAR WITH CIDER. PLACE THE TOP ON THE JAR. CUT AN 8-INCH CIRCLE OF FABRIC USING PINKING SHEARS. PLACE OVER THE TOP OF THE JAR AND SECURE WITH A RUBBER BAND. WRAP SOME CHRISTMAS BERRIES AROUND THE RUBBER BAND TO HIDE IT. PUT THE MULLING SPICES IN THE CHEESECLOTH BAG AND TIE AROUND THE JAR. ADD A TAG THAT GIVES COOKING INSTRUCTIONS. KEEP REFRIGERATED UNTIL READY TO USE.

To:

In a large saucepan or crockery cooker, combine apple juice, 3 tablespoons brown sugar, and the spice bag. Simmer for 10 minutes in saucepan or up to 2 hours in small crockery cooker. Remove spice bag before serving. Eat with a favorite Christmas cookie and take in the season.

Love,

Holiday Cocoa Mix

Shown on pages 42

What you need

- 3 cups non fat dry milk
- 2 cups sifted powdered sugar
- 1 cup powdered non dairy creamer
- ½ cup unsweetened cocoa powder
- ½ cup chocolate chips
- Miniature marshmallows

What you do

In a bowl combine dry milk, sugar, creamer, and cocoa powder. Add chocolate chips. Keep mix in covered container on shelf. To make 1 serving, place ⅓ cup mixture in a mug and add ¾ cup very hot water. Stir. Add a few marshmallows on top. Makes about 20 servings.

To:

In a large measuring cup combine ⅔ cocoa mix and 1½ cups very hot water. Stir until well blended. Divide between two mugs. Invite a friend over for a cozy chat! Merry Christmas!

Love,

Rich Christmas Coffee Mix

Shown on page 43

What you need

- ½ cup instant coffee granules
- ½ cup powdered non dairy creamer
- ⅓ cup sugar
- ¾ teaspoon ground cinnamon
- ¼ teaspoon ground nutmeg
- ⅛ teaspoon ground cardamom

What you do

Combine all ingredients and place in an airtight container For 1 serving, place 2 to 3 tablespoons coffee mix in coffee cup or mug. Add 1 cup steaming water and stir to dissolve. Makes about 10 servings.

Merry Christmas to:

For 1 serving, place 2 to 3 tablespoons coffee mix in coffee cup or mug. Add 1 cup steaming water and stir to dissolve. Sit down and enjoy the season!

Love,

Trim the Tree Together

GATHER AROUND THE
EVERGREEN TREE AND HAVE
SOME FAMILY FUN BY MAKING
YOUR CHRISTMAS TREE THE SHOWCASE
OF YOUR HOLIDAY DECORATING.
IT WON'T TAKE LONG TO MAKE SOME
HANDMADE TRIMS, SO TRY YOUR HAND
AT PAINTING PINECONES, DECORATING
COOKIE ORNAMENTS, OR BEADING SOME
PRETTY STARS. ENJOY YOUR TIME
TOGETHER AS YOU DECORATE YOUR VERY
SPECIAL HOLIDAY TREE.

Nature's Touch

LET NATURE BE THE INSPIRATION FOR BEAUTIFUL TRIMS TO GRACE YOUR EVERGREEN TREE THIS CHRISTMAS SEASON.

Antique paper birds are cut out and dusted with glitter to create **Vintage Bird Trims**, opposite. Purchase craft nests at crafts stores, gild them with gold paint, and fill them with vintage jewelry to create **Jeweled Nests**, opposite. Real pine cones decorate evergreens all year long, so this year bring them in to appear on your holiday tree. With just a little spray paint and some glitter they make **Lovely Pinecone Ornaments.** The vintage bird art is available for you to scan and cut out on page 152. Instructions for all of the ornaments are on page 70.

Christmas Cones

PRETTY PAPERS TURN INTO MAGICAL CONES WHEN THEY CHANGE FROM 2-D TO 3-D WORKS OF ART. ADD SOME RIBBON TRIMS AND FILL THEM WITH ALL THE GOODIES OF THE SEASON.

 Vintage sheet music strikes a perfect chord when you turn it into a **Musical Cone** that hangs on your Christmas evergreen. Fill the lyrical cones with money, chocolates, tiny holiday ornaments, or little music goodies.

Create stunning **Golden Cones** using simple scrapbooking papers. We chose an embossed metallic scrapbook paper with an organic design. The edges are cut using scalloped-edge decorative scissors and trimmed with golden glitter. Instructions and patterns for making the cones are on page 71.

Sweet Polka Dot Tree

FILL THEIR HEADS WITH SUGARPLUMS AND ALL KINDS
OF CANDY BY CREATING A SWEET POLKA DOT TREE.
RIBBON CANDY, CANDY NECKLACES, AND GRAPHIC
COOKIES MAKE THIS TREE A DREAM COME TRUE.

This year make your Christmas tree magically sweet with pretty **Polka Dot Cookies,** ribbon candies that hang by pastel ribbons, nostalgic candy necklaces, and oversized and colorful gerbera daisies to complete the look. The real daisies are kept fresh in their individual water tubes. Fill the tree as full as can be for more fun that you can imagine. For instructions and the recipe for making the cookies and tips on the other ornaments, see page 72.

Make it a Gift

ANYONE WOULD LOVE TO GET A BOX OF YUMMY POLKA DOT COOKIES ALL TUCKED IN SOME COLORFUL TISSUE. USE PINKING SHEARS TO CUT PASTEL TISSUE IN SQUARES JUST LARGE ENOUGH TO OVERLAP THE EDGES OF THE BOX. STACK THE COOKIES IN THE BOX AND COVER WITH THE TISSUE.

Tapestry Bag Trims

Tapestry-like fabric makes into sweet little purses that hold all kinds of Christmas treats. Make your bags to cinch tightly shut or fold over in heart shapes, circles, or pretty little squares. Choose the fabric trims that you like best to finish your **Tapestry Bag Trims**. Instructions and patterns are on page 75.

Unexpected Twists

THE MOST COMMON SUPPLIES CAN BE EASILY
TRANSFORMED INTO BEAUTIFUL TRIMS FOR YOUR
HOLIDAY TREE WITH JUST A LITTLE TWIST OF THE
IMAGINATION.

Tiny and lovely ceramic tiles combine with pretty beads and fine wire to make **Pretty Tile Trims**. Fine wires entwine the smooth tiles and twist together to meet up with the matching beads. Instructions for making these trims are on page 76.

Easy-to-use crafting metal sheets are layered, decorated with simple designs, and set off with a Christmas postage stamp to make **Magic Metal Trims**. Scrapbooking paper clips are glued together to make clever little trims that go together oh-so-quickly. Add a ribbon to finish off these **Multi-Clip Ornaments**. For instructions for the ornaments on this page, see page 73.

Christmas Stars

Make a **Sparkling Star**, below, by threading glittering beads onto wire and then twisting the wire together to make a spoke-like star. Beads, wooden stars, and pretty paint combine to make **Icicle Stars**, opposite, that hang so gently on your holiday tree. Instructions for both star projects are on pages 76-77.

Clearly Clever Christmas Balls

You'll never stop thinking of ideas for filling clear Christmas balls after you begin! Whether you make **Tiny Ornaments**, **Clear Candle Balls**, **Evergreen Trim**, **Ribbon Filled Trims**, **Glitzy Beauty**, **Fresh Flower Pretty**, or **Nativity Trim**, you'll have fun making these see-through ornaments for your tree. For instructions for making all of these trims, see page 77.

Copper Beauties

METALLIC COPPER MAKES A STUNNING DEBUT FOR CHRISTMAS
DECORATING THIS SEASON. USE COPPER ORNAMENTS OR
SIMPLE COPPER COOKIE CUTTERS TO SHOWCASE YOUR TRIMS.

Simple copper swirl-style paper clips are glued to copper-colored Christmas balls to make **Copper Swirls**—so simple that the kids will want to help.

Have your favorite recipe at your fingertips by making a **Star Recipe** to hang on your holiday tree. The cookie cutter is the frame for this clever recipe treat. Instructions for both projects are on page 78.

Stunningly Stickered Trims

Adding dimension just got easier when you use stickers of all kinds to decorate your Christmas ornaments. Spell out a name or holiday greeting with little letter stickers to create **Greeting Trims**. Stickers that look like quilling make these **Quilled Ornaments** so easy and elegant. Square jeweled stickers make these

Royal Trims easy and fun to make. Add a sewing notion—hook and loop fasteners in the shape of circles— to make bold white dots on pretty orange ornaments creating **Dotted Trims**. For complete instructions for making all of these ornaments, see page 79.

Lovely Pinecone Ornaments

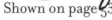

Shown on page 53

What you need

- Pinecone
- Spray paint in desired pastel color
- Glitter to match pinecone
- Ornament top from purchased ball ornament
- Strong glue such as E-6000

What you do

In a well ventilated area, spray paint the pinecone until it is well covered. You may have to spray the pinecone more than one time to completely cover it. Before the last coat dries, sprinkle it with glitter. Allow to dry. Remove the top hanger from a purchased ornament and glue to the top of the ornament. Allow to dry.

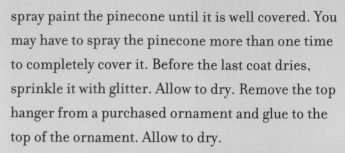

Vintage Bird Trims

Shown on page 52

What you need

- Bird images from page 152
- Cardstock
- Scissors
- Fine crafts glue
- Fine gold glitter

What you do

Scan or color copy the bird images from page 152 onto cardstock and cut out. Add a touch of glue to desired areas and dust with glitter. Tuck into the branches of the tree.

Jeweled Nests

Shown on page 52

What you need

- Purchased crafts bird nests (available at crafts stores)
- Gold spray paint
- Fine gold ribbon
- Vintage jewelry

What you do

In a well-ventilated area, spray paint the nests. Allow to dry. Tie a ribbon onto the nests and fill with vintage jewelry. Hang on the tree.

Christmas Cones

Shown on pages 54—55

What you need
- Tracing paper or photocopier
- 8x8-inch piece cardstock in desired color, or vintage sheet music
- Scissors and decorative edge scissors
- Paper punch
- Crafts glue
- Clip clothespin
- Gold glitter or ribbon trims
- Cording or ribbon for hanging

What you do

Trace or photocopy the pattern, below. Draw around the pattern onto the chosen cardstock. Cut out. Trim the curved edge with decorative-edge scissors for the gold cone. Form into a cone and glue in place. Use a clothespin to hold edges together until dry. Form the vellum cone liner in the same way. Place inside the metallic cone. Trim music cone with ribbon trims. Punch a hole in each side of the cone. Thread a ribbon or cording through the holes and tie a knot at each end for hanging.

Sweet Polka Dot Tree

Shown on pages 56—57

What you need

For the cookies

- 2½ cups all-purpose flour
- 1 teaspoon baking powder
- ½ teaspoon salt
- ¾ cup butter, softened
- 1 cup granulated sugar
- 2 eggs
- 1 teaspoon lemon extract
- 1 recipe Meringue Icing (see page 29)
- Paste food coloring (peach, pink, lavender, orange, lemon yellow, leaf green, blue, neon green, violet, fuchsia pink, golden yellow)

What you do for the cookies

In a large bowl stir together flour, baking powder and salt. In another bowl beat butter with an electric mixer. Beat in sugar until well combined and fluffy. Beat in eggs until well combined. Add lemon extract. Gradually beat in flour mixture, using a spoon if too thick for mixer. Divide dough into two portions. Wrap in plastic wrap and chill several hours or until easy to handle.

Roll out chilled dough on a lightly floured surface to about ¼ to ⅛ inch thick. Cut out shapes with cookie cutters. Use plain or crinkled round cookie cutters to shape cookies.

Place cookies 1 inch apart on lightly greased cookie sheet. Use the end of a straw to make small holes at the top of cookies for hanging. Bake in a 375 degree oven for 6 to 8 minutes or until edges just begin to brown. Let cool on cookie sheet for 2 minutes. Remove to a wire rack to cool completely. Makes about 4 dozen 3-inch cookies.

For each color icing to be tinted, place about ½ cup Meringue Icing in a small bowl. Keep remaining icing covered when not using. Tint icing desired colors with a small amount of paste food coloring. Use a clean artist's brush to apply a base coat of desired icing colors. Let dry several hours. Use the brush to make small or large polka dots on each cookie. Dry completely.

Thread the satin ribbon through the hole and hang on the tree.

For the ribbon candy— break the candy into pieces and hang with coordinating ribbon.

For the gerbera daisy accents— break off stem to measure about 3-inch long. Place stem into water-filled water tube and tuck into tree branches.

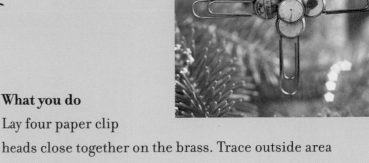

Multi Clip Ornaments

Shown on page 61

What you need

- **Scrapbooking decorative paper clips**
- **1x1-inch piece of light brass crafting metal such as Art Emboss**
- **Strong crafts glue such as Quick Grip adhesive**
- **Side cutters; metal file**
- **Scissors; pencil**

What you do

Lay four paper clip heads close together on the brass. Trace outside area of the paper clip heads onto brass with a pencil. Cut out. This piece will serve as the backing for the paper clip ornament. Trim off the brass piece around the outside edges of the paper clip heads. Glue the paper clips to the brass backing using strong crafts glue. Choose a paper clip for the center of the ornament. Cut the paper clip wires off using the side cutters. File any exposed wires ends down using a metal file. Glue the center paper clip head onto the ornament center. Let dry overnight.

Metal Magic Trims

Shown on page 61

What you need

- **3³⁄₄ x 4¹⁄₂-inch piece light aluminum crafting metal such as Art Emboss**
- **3¹⁄₄ x 4-inch piece light copper crafting metal such as Art Emboss**
- **2¹⁄₄ x 3-inch piece green scrapbook paper**
- **1³⁄₄ x 2¹⁄₂-inch piece gold scrapbook paper**
- **Santa postage stamp**
- **Piece of craft foam**
- **Double-sided tape**
- **Stylus or ball point pen**
- **¹⁄₂ inch hole punch**
- **Ruler; pencil; scissors**
- **Ribbon for hanging**

What you do

Layer the pieces atop each other and mark where they overlap. Decorate or "tool" the metal pieces only where they will show. "Tool" the metal pieces by making designs using the stylus. Lay the metal pieces on top of a piece of craft foam (the craft foam serves as a nice, soft surface for tooling metal), and simply draw designs on the metal. Turn it over when you like the result. Layer the pieces starting with the aluminum on the bottom, ending with the stamp. Hold them together using double sided tape. Punch a hole in each side at the top. Hang with ribbon.

73

Tapestry Bag Trims

Shown on pages 58–59

What you need
(for 4 bags of any style)

- **Tracing paper; pencil**
- **½ yard of lightweight tapestry-like fabric in desired color**
- **Lining fabric in color to match main fabric**
- **Sewing thread to match fabric color**
- **Scissors**
- **Cording**

What you do
For Drawstring Pouch Bag
Cut two 8-inch circles, one each from lining fabric and outside fabric. With right sides together, sew together, using a ¼-inch seam, leaving opening about 1½ -inch long for turning. Clip curves, turn, and press. Slipstitch opening closed.

Stitch through both layers ⅜-inch from outside edge. Stitch again ¾-inch from edge making a casing for cording. Clip hole through only outside layer of fabric at 2 points in center of stitching to draw cord through. Draw 1 or 2 cords about 16 inches in length through casing. (If using one string, make only one hole.) Sew tassels, beads or ribbon flowers to ends of cording, or tie cording in knots.

For Flap Pouch (Pattern A1 and A2)
Trace or copy patterns. Cut one A1 pattern piece each from outside fabric and lining. Cut one A2 pattern piece from outside fabric. On A2 pattern piece, fold over ¼-inch twice on top edge and stitch, forming a rolled hem for top edge. On piece A1, with right sides together, stitch lining fabric to outside fabric between lines around curved edge, backstitching at lines marked, using ¼-inch seam. Clip curve, turn, and press.

With right sides together, sew A1 to A2 pieces from turned curved edge of A1, down sides and across bottom using ¼-inch seam. For fringe or beading at bottom edge, baste trim to A2 bottom edge before sewing pieces together. Clip corners diagonally, turn, and press.

Cut cording handle to approximately 7 inches. Sew at corners of flap. Sew trim to flap curved edge if desired. Close flap with button/buttonhole or snap closure and button or trim on top.

For Heart Pouch (Pattern B) and Curved Flat Pouch (Pattern C)
Trace or copy patterns. Cut 2 each from fabric and contrasting lining from pattern piece B or C. Baste handle (approximately a 6-8-inch piece of cording) to right side of one lining piece at top side corner, having cut edge of cording at top and length extending down. With right sides together, stitch each set of lining and fabric pieces together at top edge from side marking, across top to marking on opposite side, using ¼-inch seam. Clip curved edges.

Turn right side out and press. With right sides together, stitch 2 pieces together at side and lower edges starting and stopping at top edges where top turned edge began, using ¼-inch seam. Turn right side out and press.

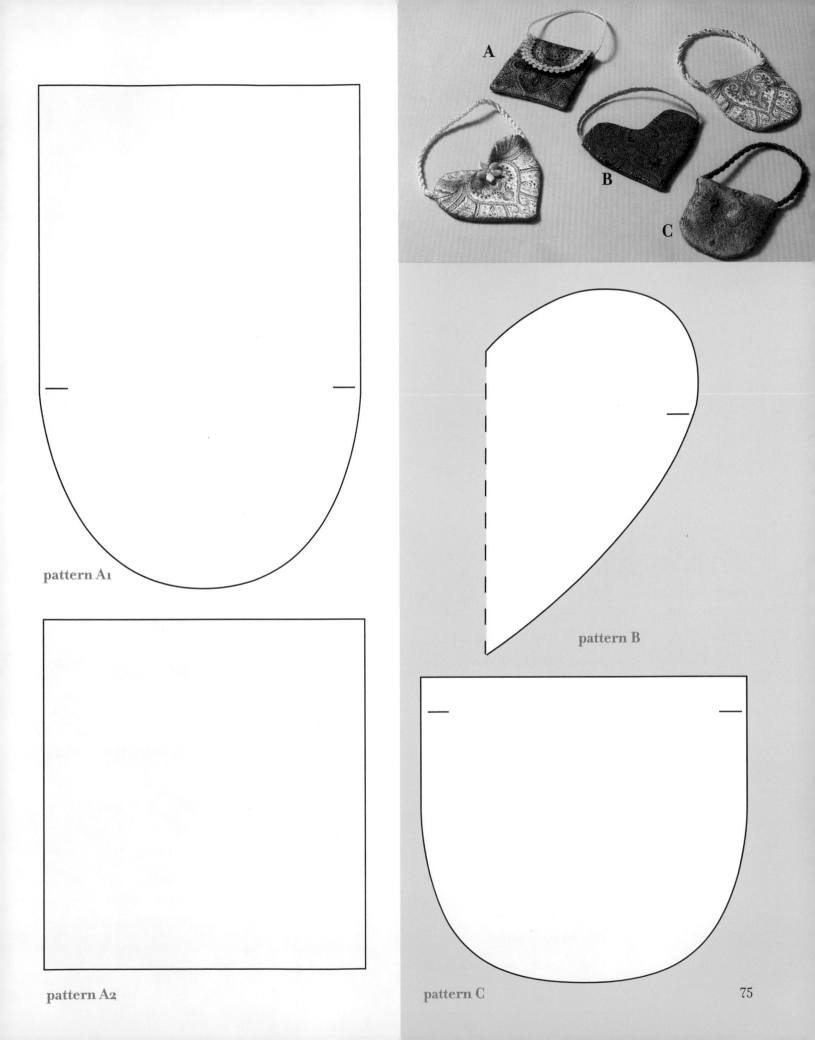

pattern A1

pattern A2

pattern B

pattern C

75

Pretty Tile Trims

Shown on page 60

What you need

- Ceramic tiles
- Acrylic paint to match tile color
- Paintbrush
- Ruler
- 20 gauge silver beading wire
- Wire cutters
- Assorted decorative glass beads
- Needle nose pliers

What you do

Paint back of ceramic tiles and let dry. (If necessary, remove glue backing from tiles.)

Measure and cut a piece of wire two feet long. Bend in half forming a small loop at one end. Wrap one of the wire ends around the other to secure a loop. Thread two decorative glass beads on the two wires. Wrap wires around tile down the sides and around the bottom of tile. Twist wires together on the backside of tile periodically to secure.

Bend one of the remaining wires down the bottom corner of tile and thread remaining decorative glass beads. Coil wire end using needle nose pliers.

Icicle Stars

Shown on page 63

What you need

- Wood round and oval beads
- Wood stars
- Acrylic paint in jewel colors such as green, fuchsia, and purple
- Gold leaf
- Gold leaf adhesive
- 20 gauge gold wire
- Assorted gold and glass beads
- Side cutters
- Long nose pliers
- Round nose pliers
- Crafts knife; ruler; paint brush

What you do

Locate the center of the wood stars and puncture a hole using a craft knife on a protected surface. Paint wood beads and stars. Let dry thoroughly. Apply gold leaf adhesive according to manufacturer's directions. Apply gold leaf brushing away excess gold leaf as directed. Measure and cut one piece of wire eight inches long. Coil one inch of one end of wire using round nose pliers. Begin threading gold beads, glass beads, and wood pieces. Bend a small loop at the top of the ornament with the remaining wire. Wrap the excess wire around the base of the loop to secure. Cut off excess wire.

Sparkling Star

Shown on page 62

What you need

- 20 gauge crafting wire
- Wire cutter
- Needlenose pliers
- Assorted beads with holes large enough to fit over wire
- Ribbon for hanging

What you do

Cut the wire into four 6-inch pieces. Use the wire snips to curve the end of the wire just enough to keep the beads from falling off. Thread an even number of beads on the wires leaving the beads loose enough for a ½ inch gap in the middle. Twist the wires together in the middle forming a star. Add a ribbon for hanging if desired.

Clearly Clever Christmas Balls

Shown on pages 64—65

What you need

For all the balls

- Clear glass ornaments in desired size and shape with removable top hangers— available at crafts and discount stores

What you do

Ribbon-Filled Trims—remove top and fill ball with tiny stick-on bows. Replace top and add ribbon for hanging.

Clear Candle Balls— remove top and fill with birthday candles. Replace top; add ribbon to hang.

Evergreen Trim— remove top and fill ball with small pieces of artificial greenery and berries. Replace top and add ribbon for hanging.

Fresh Flower Pretty— remove top and fill ball with small fresh flowers. Replace top and add ribbon for hanging. Flowers will use their own moisture and should last for about 4-5 days.

Glitzy Beauty— remove top and fill ball with pieces of tinsel garland. Replace top and add a piece of vintage jewelry and ribbon for hanging.

Tiny Ornaments— remove top and fill ball with tiny Christmas ornaments. Replace top and add ribbon for hanging.

Nativity Trim— remove top and fill ball with small pieces of hay. Add a purchased nativity figure and ribbon for hanging.

Star Recipe

Shown on page 67

What you need

- **Copper cookie cutter**
- **Pencil**
- **Cream colored cardstock or large recipe card**
- **Paper punch**
- **Favorite recipe**
- **Fine tip marking pen**
- **Toothpick**
- **Strong crafts glue**
- **Narrow ribbon**

What you do

Lay the cookie cutter on the cardstock or recipe card. Draw around the cookie cutter onto the paper with a pencil. Cut out the shape and punch a little hole in the top of the paper shape. Use a fine tip pen to write the recipe inside the shape. Use the back of the shape to complete the recipe if necessary.

Use a toothpick to spread the glue on the edge of the cookie cutter. Carefully line up the shape of the paper with the edge of the cutter. Allow to dry. Put the fine ribbon through the hole for hanging.

Copper Swirls

Shown on page 66

What you need

- **Purchased copper colored ball**
- **Copper swirl paper clips**
- **Strong crafts glue**
- **Toothpick**
- **White crafts glue**
- **Copper colored fine glitter**

What you do

Carefully put glue on the back of the paper clips using the toothpick. Glue to the ball in desired design. Allow to dry. Make swirl shapes with the white crafts glue. Sprinkle with glitter.

Stunningly Stickered Trims

Shown on pages 68—69

What you need

For all the trims

- **Purchased ornament in desired color**
- **Crafts glue**
- **Fine glitter**
- **Stickers**

Here's a Crafting Secret

When you are crafting or decorating round christmas ornaments, use a drinking glass tumbler to hold the ornament while you are working on it and while it is drying. Simply prop the Christmas ball in the tumbler, work on it, and let it dry. After it is dry, turn it and work on the other side.

What you do

Greeting Trims—arrange stickers on the ball to spell holiday words or names. Use crafts glue to add dots of glitter on the ball and dust with glitter. Allow to dry.

Royal Trims— adhere jeweled stickers on the ball in desired arrangement. Use crafts glue to outline the stickers and dust with glitter.

Quilled Ornaments—arrange 3-D quilled stickers on the ball in the center. Use glue and glitter to make glitter ribbons connecting the stickers. Allow to dry.

Dotted Trims— arrange sewing hook and loop fasteners such as Velcro on the ball. Use glue to outline the Velcro dots and dust with glitter. Allow to dry.

Stir Up Some Homemade Goodies

WONDERFUL SCENTS FILL THE AIR AS YOU GATHER IN THE KITCHEN TO CELEBRATE THE SEASON. PREPARE YOURSELF FOR SMILES OF ANTICIPATION AND HUGS OF GRATITUDE WHEN YOU PRESENT THEM WITH GOODIES YOU MADE JUST FOR THEM.

Santa Claus Cookies

Whether you are making a Santa star, a Santa moon, a Santa circle, or any other cookie that features the Jolly Old Elf, you'll love the look when you use colors that have a vintage appeal. The recipe and tips for decorating these **Santa Claus Cookies** are on page 94.

Make it a Gift

MAKE A WISH TO SANTA COME TRUE BY PACKING A FEW SANTAS INTO A LITTLE PARCHMENT SACK. PURCHASE THE SACKS AT A BAKERY OR A SCRAPBOOK STORE. CUT THE BAG IN HALF WITH PINKING SCISSORS AND PUNCH HOLES ALONG THE TOP. THREAD A RIBBON THROUGH THE HOLES AND PUT SOME SANTAS IN THE BAG FOR A GREAT GIFT TREAT.

Angel Coconut Cookies

 Covered with pure white coconut, these delightful little cookies make any cookie tray seem simply heavenly. These **Angel Coconut Cookies** have a sugar cookie base with a surprise inside and are rolled in shredded coconut. The recipe is on page 95.

Old-Fashioned Date Cookies

Sure to be a family favorite
every year, these delicious
Old-Fashioned Date Cookies
are filled with chopped dates
and sweet raisins and
surrounded with a sugar cookie
dough that is rich and tender.
Fill them with our traditional
date-raisin filling or create
your own family favorite. The
recipe is on page 95.

Perfect Brownie

Treat this brownie like a piece of
artwork—it deserves your highest
praise because it is indeed the
Perfect Brownie. Made with rich
chocolate chips and dusted with
powdered sugar, all you need is a
glass of milk and Santa will be
happy. The recipe is on page 96.

Sugared Popcorn Trees

 Create your own sweet forest of trees made from popcorn and covered with a sugary snow icing. These **Sugared Popcorn Trees** will make a beautiful centerpiece, or just eat them right up as a sweet Christmas treat. The recipe is on page 97.

Candied Strawberries

Combine the wonderful flavor of fresh strawberries with pure chocolate and you will have a holiday favorite—**Candied Strawberries.** Even though they look like they were created by a candy artist, you'll know how easy they are to make. The recipe and instructions are on page 97.

Cranberry Pecan Toffee

Sweet brown sugar and just a hint of tangy cranberries make this **Cranberry Pecan Toffee** one that can't be beat. The texture is crunchy and the look is irresistible. Make plenty to have on hand for the holidays and to give as gifts. The recipe is on page 98.

Make it a Gift

🌿 Fill a purchased tin pail with pieces of cranberry pecan toffee for a sweet gift. The little pails can be purchased at crafts and discount stores in a variety of colors. Use an awl to poke holes around the edge and lace a holiday ribbon through the holes to dress up the tin.

Holiday Pistachio Cake

Pretty and green and oh-so-easy to make, this **Holiday Pistachio Cake** is moist and yummy. Make it in a pretty bundt pan and drizzle with green frosting. The recipe is on page 98.

Raspberry Cream Jelly Roll

Impress your friends with this pretty **Raspberry Cream Jelly Roll** dessert
all rolled up and dressed for the holidays. We filled our cake with whipped
cream and fresh raspberries, but you can use any filling you like. The
recipe is on page 99.

Pretty Poinsettia Cupcakes

Almost too beautiful to eat, these **Pretty Poinsettia Cupcakes** are made using cake mix and rolled out gumdrops. The sugar on the gumdrops adds sparkle and makes these cupcakes little pieces of artwork. The recipe is on page 100.

Sweet Cranberry Sherbet

So beautiful to look at and so delicious to eat, our **Sweet Cranberry Sherbet** will be the star of the dessert tray.

The color is all natural and the cranberries make it a wonderful traditional flavor to compliment any holiday meal. You will appreciate this make-ahead and yummy Christmas dessert when the big day arrives. The recipe is on page 100.

Playful Animal Cookies

Who wouldn't love to play with these happy holiday fellows? Whether you prefer the **Dog and Cat Cookies** or the **Friendly Fish Friends,** every animal lover on your list will smile when they see these happy cookies made with a delicious chocolate sugar cookie dough. Just for fun, try a clever wrap to present these special friends. The recipe and tips for decorating are on page 101.

Santa Claus Cookies

Shown on pages 82–83

What you need

- 2 cups all-purpose flour
- 1 teaspoon baking powder
- ¾ cup butter, softened
- 1 cup sugar
- 1 egg
- 2 teaspoons vanilla
- 1 recipe Decorator Frosting
- **Star, triangle, circle, and Santa moon cookie cutters, see Sources page, 157**
- **Paste food coloring (pink, leaf green, sky blue, barn red), available at craft stores**
- **Disposable decorating bag with coupler and small round and/or star tips, available at discount and crafts stores**
- **Small cinnamon red hot candies or other small round candies for nose, eyes, and trims**

What you do

In a large bowl stir together flour and baking powder. In another bowl beat butter with an electric mixer. Beat in sugar until well combined and fluffy. Beat in egg until well combined. Beat in vanilla. Gradually beat in flour mixture, using a spoon if too thick for mixer. Divide dough into two portions. Wrap in plastic wrap and chill several hours or until easy to handle. Roll out chilled dough on a lightly floured surface to ¼-inch thickness. Cut out with cookie cutter and place on ungreased baking sheet. Bake in a 375 degree oven for 8 minutes or until lightly brown. Cool on wire rack. Makes 24 cookies.

For each Santa color to be tinted, place about ½ cup Decorator Frosting in a small bowl. Keep remaining icing covered when not using. Tint icing desired colors with a small amount of paste food coloring. Gradually stir in a little water, ½ teaspoon at a time, until icing is thin enough to paint on cookies. Use a clean artist's brush to paint a base coat of desired icing color onto each cookie where Santa's coat or hat will appear. Let dry about an hour. Meanwhile fit a decorating bag with a coupler and small star tip. Fill bag with some remaining white stiff icing. Pipe on fur coat trim, beard, and mustache. Use a small dot of icing to attach candy nose, eyes, and other trims.

Decorator Frosting

In a large bowl beat 1 cup shortening, 2 teaspoons clear vanilla, and ½ teaspoon almond extract. Gradually beat in 2 cups sifted powdered sugar. Beat in 2 tablespoons milk. Gradually beat in 2 cups additional powdered sugar and enough milk (2 to 3 tablespoons) to make a frosting that is creamy and holds a stiff peak. Makes about 3 cups.

Angel Coconut Cookies

Shown on page 84

Note: The same sugar cookie dough is used for both cookies on this page.

What you need

- 1 cup butter, softened
- 2 cups sugar
- 3 eggs
- 1 teaspoon vanilla
- 4 cups all-purpose flour
- ½ teaspoon salt
- Pecan halves
- White chocolate
- Shredded coconut

What you do

In a mixing bowl cream butter and sugar. Add eggs, one at a time, beating well after each addition. Beat in vanilla. Combine flour and salt and gradually add to the creamed mixture. Cover and refrigerate for 3 hours or until easy to handle. Wrap a small amount of dough around a pecan half. Form into a small ball and place on an ungreased cookie sheet. Bake at 375 degrees for 10 minutes. When cool, dip into white melted chocolate and roll in coconut. Makes 3 dozen cookies.

Old-Fashioned Date Cookies

Shown on page 85

What you need

Filling

- ½ cup sugar
- 1½ teaspoons cornstarch
- ¼ teaspoon cinnamon
- 1 cup chopped dates
- ½ cup raisins
- ½ cup water

Dough

- 1 cup butter, softened
- 2 cups sugar
- 3 eggs
- 1 teaspoon vanilla
- 4 cups all-purpose flour
- ½ teaspoon salt

What you do

In a saucepan, combine all ingredients for filling. Cook and stir over medium heat until thickened. Cool. Prepare dough as for Angel Coconut Cookies, above. Cover and refrigerate 3 hours or until easy to handle.

On a lightly floured surface roll half of the dough to ⅛-inch thickness. Cut with a 3-inch round cookie cutter. Place 1 inch apart on an ungreased baking sheet. Place 1 teaspoon of date filling in the center of each cookie. Roll out remaining dough and cut with a 3-inch cookie cutter. With a 1-inch round cookie cutter, cut a hole in the center of each cookie to place over the filling. With a fork, press edges to seal. Bake at 350 degrees for 10 to 12 minutes. Makes about 30 cookies.

Perfect Brownie

Shown on page 85

What you need

- 2 cups sugar
- 2 cups all-purpose flour
- 1 cup water
- ½ cup butter
- ½ cup vegetable oil
- 4 tablespoons cocoa
- ½ cup buttermilk
- 2 eggs
- ¾ teaspoon baking soda
- 1 teaspoon cinnamon
- 1 teaspoon vanilla
- ½ cup chocolate chips
- ½ cup chopped walnuts

What you do

Preheat oven to 375 degrees. In a large mixing bowl, combine sugar and flour. In a saucepan, combine the water, butter, vegetable oil, and cocoa. Bring to a boil. Remove from heat and pour over the flour mixture, mixing well.

Add buttermilk, eggs, soda, cinnamon and vanilla. Fold in chocolate chips and walnuts. Mix well. Pour batter into large greased jelly-roll pan and bake for about 25 minutes. Cool.

Powdered Sugar Decoration

Choose a pattern that you wish to use to make a design on top of the brownies. We have given you patterns, below, or make up a simple pattern of your own.

Copy the pattern onto clean white paper. Cut out with crafts knife or small scissors. You can decorate individual pieces of the brownie or decorate the entire pan of brownies.

Lay the pattern on the cooled cake where you want the design to be. Pour about ½ cup of powdered sugar into a sieve. Shake the sieve over the pattern until the brownie is white. Carefully remove the paper pattern.

Sugared Popcorn Trees

Shown on page 86

What you need

- **20 cups popped white kernel popcorn**
- **2 cups sugar**
- **1 cup water**
- **½ cup corn syrup**
- **1 teaspoon vinegar**
- **½ teaspoon salt**
- **2 teaspoons vanilla**
- **1 can purchased white frosting**
- **Assorted sugars and candy decorations**

What you do

Put popped popcorn in a large greased roasting pan and keep warm in a 300 degree oven while making syrup. Butter the sides of a large heavy saucepan. In saucepan combine sugar, water, corn syrup, vinegar, and salt. Cook and stir over medium-high heat until sugar dissolves. Clip a candy thermometer to side of pan. Continue to cook and stir at a boiling rate until syrup reaches 250 degrees, about 10-15 minutes. Remove from heat and remove thermometer. Stir in vanilla. Pour syrup evenly over the warm popcorn. Stir until evenly coated. When popcorn is cool enough to handle, use buttered hands to shape into 5- to 6-inch trees. Place on greased foil to cool. Wrap in plastic wrap to store up to 1 week. Just before displaying, decorate with piped frosting and candy decorations. Makes about 5 trees.

Candied Strawberries

Shown on page 86

What you need

- **1 pint fresh strawberries (not hulled)**
- **1 cup white chocolate chips**
- **1 cup dark chocolate chips**
- **Course sugar (optional)**

A

What you do

Wash strawberries and pat dry. Set aside. Place white or dark chocolate chips in small microwave-safe bowl and place in microwave for about 1½ minutes or just until melted. Stir to blend chips. Insert toothpick into strawberry and dip into melted chocolate. Cool on waxed paper and set in clean egg carton until chocolate is set. See photo A, left. Melt contrasting chocolate; drizzle on top and sprinkle with sugar if desired. Makes about 20 large strawberries.

Cranberry Pecan Toffee

Shown on page 87

What you need

- ¾ cup dried cranberries
- 1 cup butter
- 1 teaspoon vanilla
- 1 cup sugar
- 1 tablespoon corn syrup
- 3 tablespoons water
- ¾ cup chopped pecans
- ½ cup chocolate chips
- ¼ cup finely chopped pecans for topping

What you do

Butter an 8x8-inch pan and sprinkle bottom with dried cranberries. Set aside. Melt 1 cup butter with vanilla in a heavy saucepan. Blend in sugar, syrup and water. Cook over medium to high heat until mixture reaches 300 degrees on candy thermometer. Quickly stir in chopped pecans. Pour mixture into pan. Sprinkle chocolate chips on top and spread when soft. Sprinkle with finely chopped pecans. When cool, remove from pan and repeat with melted chocolate chips and nuts on the opposite side. Cool thoroughly and break into pieces.

Holiday Pistachio Cake

Shown on page 88

What you need

- 1 package 2-layer-size yellow or white cake mix
- 2 packages instant pistachio pudding mix
- ½ cup vegetable oil
- ½ cup water
- ½ cup milk
- 5 eggs

Vanilla Glaze

- 1 cup powdered sugar
- 1 teaspoon vanilla
- About 2 tablespoons hot water
- Green food coloring (optional)

What you do

Place all ingredients in large bowl of mixer. Beat at low speed until moistened. Beat 4 minutes at medium speed. Pour into greased bundt pan. Bake at 350 degrees for about 1 hour. Let set 5 minutes before removing from the pan. Cool. Spread top of cake with Vanilla Glaze, allowing some to drizzle down sides.

Vanilla Glaze

Mix powdered sugar and vanilla. Stir in enough water to reach proper glaze consistency. Add green food coloring if desired. Drizzle on cake.

Raspberry Cream Jelly Roll

Shown on page 89

What you need

- 3 eggs
- 1 cup granulated sugar
- ½ cup water
- 1 teaspoon vanilla
- ¾ cup all-purpose flour
- 1 teaspoon baking powder
- ¼ teaspoon salt
- 1 tablespoon orange juice
- Powdered sugar

Raspberry Filling

- 1 cup heavy whipping cream
- ½ cup powdered sugar
- ¾ cup washed and drained fresh red raspberries

What you do

Heat oven to 375 degrees. Line a 15x10x1-inch jelly-roll pan with waxed paper. Grease the waxed paper with non-stick vegetable spray or butter. Set aside.

In a small mixer bowl, beat eggs for about 5 minutes or until very thick. Pour eggs into large mixer bowl and gradually beat in granulated sugar. On low speed, beat in water, orange juice, and vanilla. Gradually add flour, baking powder, and salt, beating just until batter is smooth. Pour into pan, spreading batter evenly.

Bake 12 to 15 minutes or until wooden toothpick inserted in center comes out clean.

While cake is baking, prepare a clean dishtowel to roll the cake. Lay the towel flat and dust with about ½ cup powdered sugar.

While cake is still warm, loosen cake from edges of pan. Invert on towel sprinkled with powdered sugar. Carefully remove waxed paper, trimming off stiff edges, if necessary. While still warm, roll cake and towel from narrow end. Cool on wire rack.

Raspberry Filling

Beat cream with mixer until almost stiff. Add powdered sugar and continue beating until stiff. Fold in raspberries.

Unroll cake and remove towel. Spread filling onto cake and reroll the cake. Sprinkle with powdered sugar and wrap in foil until ready to slice. Makes about ten 1-inch slices.

Pretty Poinsettia Cupcakes

Shown on page 90

What you need

- **One package cake mix**
- **Ingredients to make cupcakes as indicated on the box**
- **Muffin tin**
- **Purchased vanilla frosting**
- **Red, white, and green gumdrops**
- **White non pareil-covered gumdrops**
- **Additional sugar**
- **Rolling pin**
- **Small holly-leaf cookie cutter**

What you do

Prepare cupcakes as indicated on the package. Choose a favorite cake mix to use with the vanilla frosting. For each gumdrop poinsettia you will need 5 red and/or white gumdrops, 2 or 3 green gumdrops, and one non-pareil covered gumdrop. To make poinsettia petals and leaves, on a cutting board sprinkled with sugar, roll out gumdrops to about ⅛-inch thickness. Keep gumdrop from sticking to rolling pin by sprinkling additional sugar on top of and underneath gumdrop while rolling. Use a 2-inch holly leaf cookie cutter to cut out shapes. Arrange them on frosted cupcakes. For center of flower, press a halved non-pareil gumdrop in center. Tip: Spray cookie cutter lightly with non stick vegetable spray to keep it from sticking to gumdrops when cutting.

Sweet Cranberry Sherbet

Shown on page 91

What you need

- **2 cups fresh cranberries**
- **1¼ cups water**
- **1 cup sugar**
- **1 teaspoon unflavored gelatin**
- **¼ cup cold water**
- **Juice of 1 lemon**

What you do

Cook cranberries in 1¼ cups water until skins pop. Press through sieve. Add sugar and cook until sugar dissolves. Add gelatin softened in cold water. Cool. Add lemon juice. Freeze until firm in shallow pan. Break into chunks; beat smooth with electric or rotary beater. Return quickly to cold pan. Freeze until firm. Serves 4 to 6.

Playful Animal Cookies

Shown on page s 92–93

What you need

- 1 cup butter, softened
- ⅔ cup packed brown sugar
- 1 teaspoon vanilla
- 1 egg
- 2 ¼ cups all-purpose flour
- ¼ cup cocoa powder
- **Animal cookie cutters, see Sources, page 157**
- **Meringue Icing (see page 29)**
- **Paste food coloring in desired colors**

What you do

In a large bowl beat butter for 30 seconds. Beat in brown sugar until fluffy. Beat in vanilla and egg. Beat well. In a small bowl stir together flour and cocoa powder. Gradually add to butter mixture. Beat until combined.

If necessary, cover and chill dough until easy to handle. Roll out dough on a lightly floured surface to ¼-inch thickness. Cut into desired shapes. Use a variety of dog, cat, and fish cookie cutters to shape cookies. Place 1 inch apart on ungreased cookie sheet. Bake in a 350 degree oven for about 8 minutes or until lightly browned. Remove to a wire rack to cool completely. Makes 3 to 4 dozen cookies.

For each color to be tinted, place about ½ cup Meringue Icing in a small bowl. Keep remaining icing covered when not using. Tint icing desired colors with a small amount of paste food coloring. We used the following paste colorings to make our tinted icing colors— ivory, brown, black, egg yellow, orange, violet, red, leaf green, and blue.

To decorate cookies, use a wet-on-wet technique. Working on one cookie at a time, use a clean artist's brush to paint a base color on cookie. While first icing is still wet, clean brush and apply another icing color to add details. You may add several colors of icing to get desired effect. Let iced cookies dry completely (overnight).

Decorators Tip: When working with many different icing colors over an extended period of time, it is helpful to place the small batches of tinted icing in very small disposable round containers with lids. The icings can be stored overnight in refrigerator. Stir icings before using again to restore consistency.

Surprise them with Handmade Gifts and Cards

WHETHER IT IS A HAND KNIT SCARF, A SWEET BAR OF SOAP, A PRETTY CHRISTMAS STOCKING FILLED WITH TREATS, OR A DECORATED JAR OF GINGERBREAD COOKIES, THE HANDMADE GIFTS YOU GIVE WILL BE THE FAVORITE GIFTS OF ALL. CREATE A ONE-OF-A-KIND CARD TO ACCOMPANY THESE TREASURES AND YOUR GIFT-GIVING IS COMPLETE.

Personality Soaps

Add a special touch of personality to little handmade soaps that will please everyone on your Christmas list.

Easy to make and so much fun to use, these clever soaps can be made in an evening. Put those tiny single doll shoes that seem to accumulate in the toy box to good use by adding them to some pastel pink glycerine soap creating **Little Girlie Soaps.**

For an unexpected twist, break up some peppermint candies and add to light green glycerine soap to make **Peppermint Twist Soaps.**

For the little boys or animal lover on your list, purchase some small zoo animal toys and add them to a soft yellow glycerine soap to make **Zoo-Lover Soaps.** For complete instructions for making all of the soaps, see page 122.

Wrap It!

After the soap is made, put it into a purchased corsage bag. (You can purchase the bags at floral supply stores.) Tie the top with a ribbon that matches the soap. Add a coordinating toy or candy to the ribbon.

Knit a Gift

Wrap It!

Make this Christmas gift one she'll love! Give her the hand knit poncho, the perfect jeans, a cute t-shirt to wear under the poncho, and finish off the gift with just the right sassy shoes. Wrap it all up with bright ribbon and be ready for lots of thank yous!

Who wouldn't love to receive one of these lovely hand-knitted pieces! Our multi-colored **Fashion Poncho** is so cleverly but easily made in two pieces using only the basic knit and purl stitch. The easy-to-make **Think Pink Hat and Scarf** made with hot pink fun-to-use yarn will be a wintertime favorite for years to come. Instructions for all three projects are on pages 122–123.

Gifts in a Jar

Jars aren't just for goodies from the kitchen—fill them with all kinds of gifty surprises! For a sweet new baby, make a **Baby Stocking Jar**, below, by filling a canning jar with little baby socks in the colors that suit the new arrival. Cut a circle of paper that matches the little wardrobe and tie on a gift tag.

For the world traveler, make a **Travel Jar**, right, by filling the jar with much-appreciated travel-size cosmetics. Cut a circle from an old map to top it off and add a luggage-tag gift tag and a little ornament.

The knitter on your Christmas list will love a jar of novelty yarn! Tie on some knitting needles to make this **Jar of Knitting**, right, a favorite gift.

Who says all your Christmas cookies have to be homemade? Purchase your favorites and stack them in a **Cookie Jar,** below, for easy giving. Cut a piece of brown paper for the top, trim the jar with 3-D stickers, and tie a ribbon around the top edge.

109

Felted Wool Gifts

Everyone on your Christmas list would love to have a stylish felted wool scarf or a little felted wool stocking. The **Felted Sweater Scarf**, below, recycles a cast-off sweater into a toasty warm scarf that is sure to become a fashion favorite.

Make a little **Felted Wool Stocking**, left, to hold some little gifts that just fit into this small size gift-holder. The **Color Block Scarf**, below, is made using shades of green felted wool with a simple clipped fringe. Instructions for both scarves and the little felt stocking are on pages 124—125.

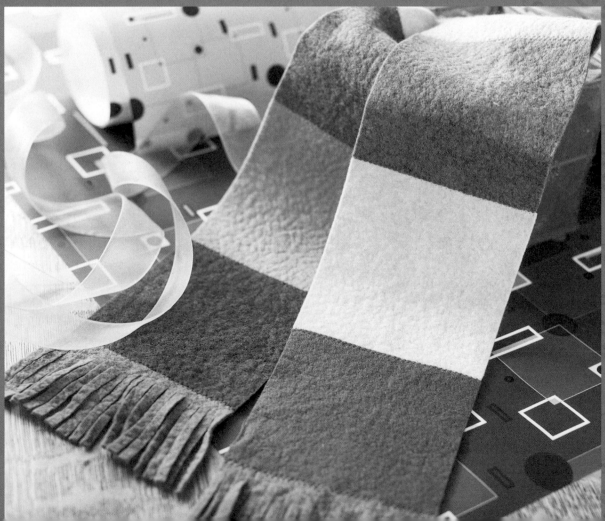

Seeing Red and Green

 If it is all about Christmas colors then these gifts are right on target! Find a clever container in just the right shade of red or green and then fill it with gifts for that special and colorful character on your list.

For our **Seeing Red** gift, right, we started with a set of red mixing bowls and then filled them with everything from a calculator to a pretty red washcloth. For the **Seeing Green** gift, below, we used a lime green purse and filled it with all kinds of green—lotions, a watch, soap and everyone's favorite—money.

Rubber Stamp Art Vases

A simple rubber stamp motif is all it takes to make a plain glass vase into **Rubber Stamp Art Vases**. Choose a holiday stamp and use glass paints to create your masterpiece. Make a simple vellum gift tag to coordinate with the vase. Instructions are on page 126.

Beautifully Beaded Jewelry

It only takes a few minutes to make a lovely beaded piece of jewelry that will be treasured forever. Our **Two-Stranded Necklace** uses pretty red and silver beads. The **Classic Pink** necklace leaves some wire showing for a sophisticated look. The **Cool Greens Bracelet** uses monochromatic tones of green to create a stunning look. Instructions for all the beaded projects are on page 126.

Wrap It !

For a clever wrap, use a vintage Christmas hankie to nest your beautiful jewelry in. Fold the hankie and tuck it into a champagne glass and then gently slide the jewelry into the hankie. Add a bow around the base of the glass to finish the look.

Retro Holiday Stocking

Our **Retro Holiday Stocking** was sewn from vintage curtain fabric found at a flea market. The angled cuff adds some 60s style to this fun stocking. Fill it with fun, unexpected collectibles. For instructions and patterns to make the stocking, see page 127.

Arty Decoupage Boxes

 **Arty Decoupage Boxes** are so fun to make and you can choose the color and pattern of paper to fit the gift you are giving. Find the papers you love and decoupage them to a purchased cardboard box in the shape that fits. Instructions for making these cool boxes are on page 128.

 Use your favorite holiday motifs to make the perfect card for everyone on your list. Our Christmas **Tree Card**, right, is created using purchased stickers and a hint of glitter. The **Candy Joy Card**, below, is perfect for the sweet-tooth on your list. Make it in just a few minutes using the exclusive art on page 153.

Make **Winter Cards**, left, to be treasured all season long. Make a pop-up style **Peace Card** that is so beautiful yet easy to make using a quick folding technique. The **Snowflake Card** simply uses snowflake eyelets to decorate the front of the card.

Make a **Vintage Santa Card**, below, in the old-world spirit using the beautiful and exclusive art provided on page 155.

Instructions for making all of the greeting cards are on pages 128—129.

Elizabeth recommends

Ginger bread

Our Favorite
Christmas Cookies

Gingerbread men with
icing rick-rack.
Butterscotch cookies
in a neat stack.
Candy cane cookies with
white stripes and red.
Visions of sugar plums
dance overhead.
Christmas cookies and
holiday hearts,
that is the way the
season starts!

Make a sweet **Christmas Recipe Scrapbook**, opposite, featuring pictures of the whole family with a favorite recipe. The little 8x8-inch size makes it a perfect gift.

They'll think you are the clever one when you present them with a **Paper Bag Scrapbook**, left and below. The fun-to-make book is created using simple paper bags and little pieces of ribbon. Instructions for both scrapbooking ideas are on pages 130—131.

Sweet Gift Soaps

Shown on page 104–105

What you need

- **Block of glycerine soap in desired color (available at crafts and discount stores)**
- **Glass measuring cups**
- **Microwave**
- **Small items to put in soaps**
- **Soap mold**

What you do

Cut up the soap into small pieces or cubes about 1x1-inch in size and place in the measuring cup. Set aside. Arrange the small pieces that you want to "float" in the soap in the bottom of the mold. You can use purchased soap molds or small pans or bowls. Place the cubed soap in the microwave and heat until just melted. Skim off the top if a film develops and then pour into the molds. Let set until firm and cold—at least 4 hours or overnight. Take out of the mold.

Fashion Poncho

Shown on page 106 **Skill Level: Easy**

Skill Level: Easy
FINISHED SIZE
Width (across widest portion) = 31"
Length (from V-Neck to Point) = 21"

GAUGE
Holding 1 strand of each yarn together, in Body Pattern, 12 sts and 16 rows = 4"/10 cm.
TAKE TIME TO CHECK YOUR GAUGE.

ABBREVIATIONS
K = knit
P = purl
St(s) = stitch(es)
WS = wrong side

What you need

- **NOTE: Both yarns used in this poncho are available from Coats & Clark.**
- **Moda Dea, Kickx, Art. R102, 73% nylon/27% acrylic yarn (50 gram/1.76 ounce/71 yard ball): 7 balls of Color 3780**
- **Red Heart LusterSheen, Art. E721, 100% acrylic yarn (113 gram/4 ounce/335 yard skein): 2 skeins of Hot Pink (0735)**
- **Size 11 (8 mm) knitting needles or size needed to obtain gauge**
- **Yarn needle**

What you do
FIRST SECTION

Each Section should measure 15" wide x 30" long. Holding 1 strand of each yarn together, cast on 45 sts.
Body Pattern
Row 1 (WS): K3; (p3, k3) across. Row 2: Knit. Repeat Rows 1-2 for Body Pattern to approximately 30" from beginning, ending with a WS row. Bind off loosely.

SECOND SECTION

As for First Section.

FINISHING

Place a marker on the right side of First Section in center of one long edge. Sew short side of Second Section to First Section from marker to corner. Place a marker on the right side of Second Section in center of inside edge. Sew the short side of First Section (B) to Second Section (B) from marker to corner.

Think Pink Hat and Scarf

Shown on page 107 **Skill Level: Easy**

What you need for the hat

- **Moda Dea, Tiara, Art. R110, 100% polyester yarn (50 gram/1.76 ounce/49 yard ball): 1 ball of Pinkie (4927)**

- **Moda Dea, Dream, Art. R113, 57% nylon; 43% acrylic yarn (50 gram/1.76 ounce/98 yard ball): 1 ball of Pink (3705)**

- **Size 7 (4.5 mm) circular needle, 16" length**

- **Size 7 (4.5 mm) double point needles (dpns)**

- **Size 10 (6 mm) circular needle**

- **Yarn needle**

- **Ring-type stitch marker**

GAUGE: In Stockinette Stitch (knit every rnd) with smaller needle, 18 sts and 28 rnds = 4"/10 cm.

TAKE TIME TO CHECK YOUR GAUGE.

What you need for the scarf

- **Moda Dea, Tiara, from Coats & Clark, Art. R110, 100% polyester yarn (50 gram/1.76 ounce/49 yard ball): 3 balls of Pinkie (4927)**

- **Size 10 (6 mm) knitting needles or size needed to obtain gauge**

GAUGE: In Garter St (knit every row), 13 sts and 17 rows = 3"/7.6 cm.

TAKE TIME TO CHECK YOUR GAUGE.

What you do for the hat

SIZE: 21½" around and 6½" deep

Beginning at the lower edge with larger circular needle and Tiara, cast on 96 sts. Being careful not to twist the sts, place a marker to indicate beg of rnd and join. K9 rnds. Leaving a tail to weave in later, cut Tiara. Change to smaller circular needle and Dream. Knit 37 rnds.

Crown Shaping

Rnd 1: (SKP, k12, k2tog) 6 times.
Rnd 2: K84.
Rnd 3: (SKP, k10, k2tog) 6 times.
Rnd 4: K72.
Rnd 5: (SKP, k8, k2tog) 6 times. Change to dpns. Arrange sts onto dpns with 20 sts on each of 3 needles. **Rnd 6:** K60. **Rnd 7:** (SKP, k6, k2tog) 6 times. **Rnd 8:** K48. **Rnd 9:** (SKP, k4, k2tog) 6 times.
Rnd 10: K36. **Rnd 11:** (SKP, k2, k2tog) 6 times.
Rnd 12: K24. **Rnd 13:** (SKP, k2tog) 6 times.
Rnd 14: K12. **Rnd 15:** (K2tog) 6 times – 6 sts rem.

Leaving an 8" tail, cut yarn. Thread tail into yarn needle and back through rem 6 sts. Secure tail on WS of fabric. Weave in all loose ends on WS of fabric.

What you do for the Scarf

SIZE:
Approximately 3" x 68"

NOTES: When adding a new ball of yarn, tie the ends and continue knitting. Weave in loose ends along one side after all knitting is completed.

Cast on 3 sts.

Row 1: K3. **Row 2:** K-inc, k1, k-inc. **Row 3:** K5. **Row 4:** K-inc, k3, k-inc. **Row 5:** K7. **Row 6:** K-inc, k5, k-inc. **Row 7:** K9.
Row 8: K-inc, k7, k-inc. **Row 9:** K11. **Row 10:** K-inc, k9, k-inc.
Row 11: K13. Knit every row for Garter St until piece measures approximately 66½" long.
Row 1: K2tog, k9, k2tog. **Row 2:** K11. **Row 3:** K2tog, k7, k2tog.
Row 4: K9. **Row 5:** K2tog, k5, k2tog. **Row 6:** K7. **Row 7:** K2tog, k3, k2tog. **Row 8:** K5. **Row 9:** K2tog, k1, k2tog. **Row 10:** K3.
Last Row: Bind off.

ABBREVIATIONS
K = knit
K-inc = knit in front and back of next stitch
K2tog = knit two stitches together
Rem = remaining
Rnd = round
SKP = with yarn on wrong side of fabric, slip one stitch purlwise, knit one stitch, pass the slipped stitch over the knit stitch
St(s) = stitch(es)
WS = wrong side

Color Block Scarf

Shown on page 111

What you need

- Ten 5-inch square blocks of wool felt in desired colors that have been "felted"
- Two 3x5-inch pieces of "felted" wool felt for ends
- Sewing thread
- Scissors

What you do

"Felt" the wool felt as instructed, opposite. Allow to dry. Press. Cut into 5-inch-blocks. Press again. Align 5-inch square blocks together in one continuous row. Use a sewing machine or hand stitch to sew together using small zig-zag stitches. Make sure that the stitches cross over to both sides of each block securing them together. Add the end pieces in the same manner. Form fringe by cutting ½-inch strips up to stitching on end pieces.

Felted Sweater Scarf

Shown on page 110

What you need

- 5-inch-wide pieces of wool felt in various lengths in assorted colors that have been "felted"
- Old wool sweater with buttons and pockets
- Scissors
- Sewing thread

Note: The scarf was made by combining pieces of felted wool felt and pieces of an old wool sweater that was also "felted". The pieces were cut 5-inches wide and at varying lengths to equal approximately 58 inches.

What you do

"Felt" the wool felt and old sweater as instructed, opposite. Allow to dry. Press. Cut into 5-inch-wide pieces of various lengths—about 7 or 8 inches long. Press again. Cut the sweater into 5-inch-wide strips of varying lengths. Lay out the pieces of the felted wool and felted sweater to equal a length of about 58 inches. Use ribbing sections and button trim pieces of sweater for ends instead of fringe. Zig-zag together as for Color Block Scarf, above. Transfer pocket from sweater to lower section of felt. Add the pockets and ribbing in the same way using a zig-zag stitch.

Felted Wool Stocking

Shown on page 111

What you need

- **Tracing paper**
- **Pencil**
- **Scissors**
- **⅓ yard of felted wool in main color**
- **Scraps of felted wool for stocking cuff**
- **Embroidery floss**
- **Sewing thread to match fabric**

What you do

Trace or photocopy pattern, left, and cut out. Trace around the pattern pieces onto the felted wool and cut out. Cut strips of contrasting wool felt for cuff. Cut a 6x½-inch strip for the stocking loop for hanging.

Join contrasting strips for cuff together by aligning long straight edges together and zig-zag stitching over both edges. Use 2 strands of embroidery floss and add decorative stitches down center lines.

Fold loop in half and stitch to inside right corner of stocking back.

Make running stitches using 3 strands of embroidery floss along stocking toe and heel lines. Place stocking top along top edge of stocking front and stitch along top edge.

With wrong sides together, stitch together stocking front to stocking back, using 3 strands of embroidery floss to form closed buttonhole stitch around side and bottom edges, leaving top open.

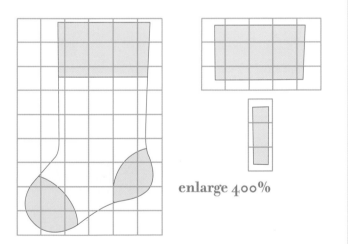

enlarge 400%

How to Felt Wool

All of the felted wool projects shown are made by first "felting" the wool pieces. Purchase wool felt at a fabric store in the desired color or colors. Wash the entire piece if you are planning to "felt" all of it. If not, cut a piece at least 1½ times larger than the size of the fabric called for. The piece will shrink when washed. Wash the wool felt or old wool sweater in hot water and dry on high heat. This will shrink the wool and give it the wrinkled or "felted" texture that you want for the projects.

Rubber Stamped Art Vases

Shown on page 113

What you need

- **Purchased glass vase**
- **Glass paint suitable for painting on glass**
- **Disposable plate**
- **Paintbrush**
- **Purchased rubber stamp**

What you do

Be sure the glass vase is clean and dry. Decide where you want to add design to the vase. Place a little paint on the plate. Use the brush to move it around on the plate until it is smooth. Dip the stamp into the paint and stamp onto the glass. Allow to dry and follow manufacturer's instructions for curing.

Beaded Jewelry

Shown on pages 114—115

What you need

- **Beads in desired colors**
- **Crimp beads**
- **Jewelry finding closures**
- **Beading wire**
- **Wire snips**
- **Crimping tool or needlenose pliers**
- **Piece of felt**

What you do

For the Two-Stranded Necklace, cut two 18-inch pieces of wire. Loop them both through one end of the closure. Thread the crimp bead on both wires and crimp to secure. String the beads in the order desired, stringing on each wire

separately. Add other end of closure finding to both wires, securing with crimp bead. Trim wires.

For the Classic Pink necklace, cut a 20-inch piece of wire. Secure one end of the finding with a crimp bead. Add one single bead and then one crimp bead to keep in place. Leave 6 inches of wire with no beads. Add a crimp bead and string 6 more inches of beads as desired. Add a crimp bead to secure. Leave wire without beads for 6 inches. Add crimp bead, single bead, crimp bead, and finding to finish. Trim wires.

For Cool Greens Bracelet, cut a 9-inch piece of wire. Secure one end of finding with crimp bead. String beads and secure other end to finish. Trim wires.

Here's a Crafting Secret

LAY BEADS ON A PIECE OF FELT IN THE ORDER YOU PLAN TO STRING THEM. THIS WILL PREVENT THEM FROM ROLLING AND ALSO KEEP THEM IN THE ARRANGEMENT YOU WANT.

Retro Holiday Stocking

Shown on page 116

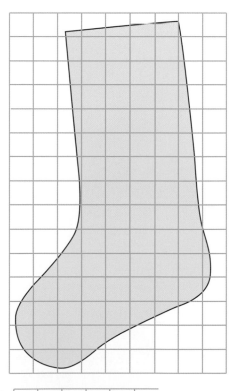

What you need

- **Tracing paper**
- **Pencil**
- **Scissors**
- **½ yard of vintage or reproduction fabric**
- **½ yard of lining fabric**
- **¼ yard of contrasting fabric for cuff**
- **Sewing thread to match fabrics**

What you do

Enlarge and trace pattern, below, left. Trace around the stocking pattern onto the vintage fabric and the lining fabric. Make two of each. Cut out. Lay the cuff pattern on the fold of the contrasting fabric and cut two cuffs. Cut a 1x8-inch strip from the contrasting fabric for the loop for hanging.

With right sides together, pin stocking fabric pieces together and sew around outside edge. Turn right side out and press. With right sides together, pin lining fabric pieces and sew around outside edge. Turn right side out and press. Slip lining inside stocking. Baste around top edge.

For hanging loop, turn under ¼-inch on both side of strip. Fold strip in half with edges even and stitch. With short edges together, lay the loop inside the stocking and baste in place.

Sew cuff pattern together along angled side. Turn and press. Use straight stitches on machine or by hand to add decorative stitching lines on the cuff. With right sides together, pin short end of cuff and stitch. With right sides together, put cuff inside stocking matching raw edges. Stitch around stocking top catching loop in the stitching. Turn cuff to outside, pull loop up, and press.

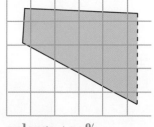

enlarge 400%

Arty Decoupage Boxes

Shown on page 117

What you need

- Purchased cardboard wrapping box
- Patterned paper in desired pattern and color
- Scissors
- Decoupage medium
- Paint brush

What you do

Cut or tear the paper into small pieces. Working on one area at a time, paint a layer of decoupage medium on the box. Layer the paper pieces on the wet medium. Continue until all the box is covered. Paint another layer on the top. Allow to dry. Paint another layer on top of the dry layer. Allow to dry.

Vintage Santa Card

Shown on page 119

What you need

- 12x7–inch piece of dark red cardstock
- 6¼ x 4⅞-inch piece of tan cardstock
- Santa art from page 155
- Glue stick; crafts glue
- Animal charms

What you do

Score the dark red cardstock in half and fold. Center and glue the tan cardstock on top of the dark red cardstock. Cut out the Santa art and glue on top of the tan cardstock. Use crafts glue to glue the animal charms around the edge.

Tree Card

Shown on page 118

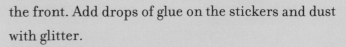

What you need

- 8x5-inch piece of blue cardstock
- Circle 3-D letter stickers
- 3-D tree stickers
- Fine green glitter
- Crafts glue

What you do:

Score and fold the cardstock in half. Spell "NOEL" with the letter stickers. Adhere the tree stickers randomly on the front. Add drops of glue on the stickers and dust with glitter.

Candy Joy Card

Shown on page 118

What you need

- 8½x5¾-inch piece of light green cardstock
- 2½x5¾-inch piece of red cardstock
- Joy candy art from page 153
- Pinking shears
- Glue stick

What you do

Score the light green paper in half and fold. Trim the red paper using the pinking shears. Scan or color copy the Joy Art on page 153 and cut out using pinking shears. Glue the red paper on the green paper. Glue the JOY letters on top of the red paper.

Winter Cards

Shown on page 119

What you need for the Peace Card

- 7x7–inch piece of blue lightweight cardstock
- Scissors; pencil
- Rectangular paper doily
- Glue stick
- Metal scrapbooking letters

What you need for the Snowflake card

- 8x6–inch piece of blue cardstock
- Pencil
- Eyelet tool
- 6 snowflake eyelets

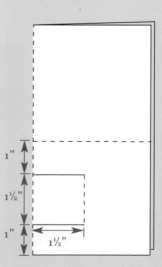

What you do

To make the pop-up Peace Card, score, and fold the cardstock in half. Fold in half again. Open and mark the cutting lines on the card referring to the diagram, below.

Cut along lines. Open up card, refold the opposite way, and pop out front of card. Cut doily to fit top and bottom of card. Glue to card. Glue letters to pop-out part of card.

For the Snowflake Card, score and fold the cardstock in half. Use a pencil to mark where eyelets are to be placed. Using the eyelet tool, place the eyelets at the marks.

1"
1½"
1"
1½"

Christmas Recipe Scrapbook

Shown on page 120

What you need

- **Cardstock**
- **Ink Stamp Pad**
- **Glue stick**
- **Scissors or straight cutter**
- **Ribbon**
- **Crafts Glue**

What you do

This 8x8-inch format scrapbook shows favorite family recipes along with photos of the family. We created our pages using 8x8-inch pieces of medium green cardstock and layered shades of green papers with Christmas red accents. Small pieces of ribbon were knotted and added to each page along with favorite 3—D stickers.

Use one or two shades of green cardstock with the same red tone throughout to keep book color design consistent.

Cut squares and round the corners to mat the stickers. Ink the edges of the mat before adhering the stickers.

Use die cut letters to make the headings of each page all look similar as in a book.

Photocopy the recipe that is featured on the original recipe card and cut out. Adhere it to the large color block area.

For cover page, cut a 6½-inch square border frame, ¼-inch wide to frame the poem and stickers.

Modify a poem or write one that fits your story. Print, cut out, and ink around the edges.

Paper Bag Book

Shown on page 121

Note: Lunch bags are not acid free. Because of this, duplicate photos or copies should be used for this project. This design will produce five 2-page layouts (10 pages) plus 3 bag openings for additional pages.

What you need

- **3 lunch bags**
- **Scoring tool**
- **Pencil**
- **Hole punch**
- **Ribbon**

What you do

Lay the first bag flat with the bottom flap of the bag facing up and to the left. Lay the next bag on top of the bottom bag with the bottom flap facing down and on the right. Lay the third bag on top of the other two bags with the bottom flap facing up and to the left. Fold all bags together to the middle. Mark positions for holes down the folded side of the book. Use a hand hole punch to create holes in one bag at a time. Add a strip of cardstock or patterned paper to the front to decorate where the holes have been punched. Once the holes are punched, tie the book together with ribbons.

Use a theme such as the 12 Days of Christmas to make it easy to tie the theme of the pages together.

Select photos to match the theme. Use duplicates or reduced-size copies.

Don't forget that a hidden "page" or tag can be placed in each of the three bag openings.

Adhere pieces in place with a strong adhesive. Adhere ribbons with glue dots or staples.

Choose materials that coordinate and create simple designs by layering 2-4 colors of cardstock with a patterned paper.

Entertain in Holiday Style

WHETHER YOU HAVE THEM OVER FOR A FANCY HOLIDAY DINNER OR JUST FOR A CASUAL LUNCHEON OR SOUP SUPPER, MAKE YOUR GET-TOGETHER ONE THEY'LL REMEMBER. DRESS UP THE TABLE WITH SIMPLE HANDMADE FAVORS, CREATE CENTERPIECES THAT SHIMMER AND SPARKLE, AND SET THE MOOD WITH CANDLES THAT GLOW. ENTERTAIN IN YOUR OWN HOLIDAY STYLE.

Pieced 9-Patch Squares

Use wool felt in colors of the season with an unexpected dash of purple trim to make pretty **Pieced 9-Patch Squares**. The pieces are "felted" first and then put together like a simple quilt block. Instructions are on page 146.

Old World Santa Placecard

Set the table in vintage style by making your own **Old World Santa Placecards**. Make one for everyone at your holiday table using the exclusive art on page 153. Instructions for making the cards on page 147.

 Clear glass light fixtures rest nicely on a clear candle base to create lovely **Light Shade Candleholders**. Add some pretty ornaments at the base to finish the look.

Choose your favorite red or green candle and then surround it with sparkling beads to make the **Beaded Beauty Candles** for your holiday table. Instructions for the candles are on pages 147 and 148.

 **Monogramed Goblets,** opposite, are so easy to make and help your guests find their own special drink.

Make your holiday soft and pretty by creating a **Snowflake Illusion**, above, at the table. Just slide a pretty snowflake between two plates for this simple look. Instructions are on pages 148 and 149.

Fairest-of-all Placecard

Tiny beveled mirrors painted with glass paints become **Fairest-of-All Placecards** that are sure to bring them to your holiday table. Paint a little motif on the mirror to make it reflect your holiday spirit. Instructions are on page 150.

Fortune Cookie Fun

Treat your guests to a look into the future while they enjoy a sweet holiday surprise. You'll love making clever **Fortune Cookie Treats** and a beautiful **Fortune Cookie Wreath**.

Dipped in pretty green candy coating, everyone will enjoy good fortune. For instructions see page 150.

Fruit-Decked Holiday Candles

The candles may be lovely and scented, but you can add your own natural touch by surrounding the candle with dried fruits that match the glorious candle color. Choose a striped candle with some deep red tones and accent it with dried cranberries for a rich **Pretty Cranberry Candle.** Place the candle in a round pressed glass dish.

Tiny dried blueberries surround a large deep-purple candle making it seem almost like a **Christmas—Past Candle**. Place it in a horizontal glass dish for display.

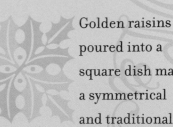 Golden raisins poured into a square dish make a symmetrical and traditional statement that creates a lovely holiday centerpiece. Place the **Golden Candle** centerpiece on a piece of pretty wrapping paper to complete the look.

Dried apricots repeat the round shape of this rich large orange candle creating a **Warm Glow Candle**. Place the candle on a glass plate and then pile the apricots around it making a rich and glorious holiday look.

Heavenly Napkin Rings

Pretty little angels get a dusting of glitter to create **Heavenly Napkin Rings**. Use the exclusive art on page 154 to make your special napkin holders. Instructions are on page 151.

Chocolate Lover's Placecard

Create the sweetest table setting placecard by making a **Chocolate Lover's Placecard**. A purchased fluted chocolate candy cup is filled with sugar and becomes the holder for the name of each special guest at your table. For instructions see page 151.

Pieced 9-Patch Squares

Shown on page 134

What you need

- ¼ yard red wool felt
- ¼ yard light green wool felt
- ¼ year medium green wool felt
- Scissors
- Monofilament sewing thread
- Purple embroidery floss

Note: Finished place mat measures 12x12 inches. Finished coasters measure 3¾ x 3¾-inches.

What you do

Wash each color of wool felt separately in hot water. Dry in hot dryer. Iron flat. (See page 125 for How to Felt Wool.)

For the place mat, cut nine 4x4-inch squares from the pre-washed and dried wool felt. Cut 4 from medium green, 3 from red, and 2 from light green. Lay the pieces in the order desired or refer to the photograph on page 134.

Butt the edges together and use the zig zag stitch on a sewing machine to sew down the center so that part of the stitch goes on either side of both squares. Add decorative stitches on top of the zig zag if desired using 3-plies of embroidery floss. Outline the outside edges with buttonhole stitch. *Note:* The pieces may be stitched together by hand rather than using a sewing machine. Simply butt up the pieces and sew back and forth across the pieces using a zig zag hand stitch. Make the coasters in the same way using nine 1¼-inch squares.

Old World Santa Placecard

Shown on page 135

What you need

- **Art from page 153**
- **Ruler**
- **Scissors**
- **8x3½-inch piece of dark green cardstock**
- **Pinking shears**
- **White crafts glue**
- **Fine green glitter**
- **Gold marking pen**

What you do

Photocopy or scan the Santa art on page 153. Cut out. Set aside.

Measure 3½-inches from one short side of the green cardstock. Mark and score the paper. Measure 3½-inches from that line and mark and score again. Fold on all scored lines. The card will stand up with 1-inch to fold under.

Using the glue stick, glue the Santa art to the front of the place card. Trim the sides with the pinking shears. Run a fine line of glue around the front of the card and dust with glitter.

Write the name of the guest on the card front with gold marker.

Light Shade Candleholder

Shown on page 136

What you need

- **Clear glass light fixture (available at home centers)**
- **Square glass candle holder**
- **Votive candle**
- **Small Christmas ornaments**

What you do

Place the votive candle on the square glass candleholder. Put the light fixture upside down over the candle. Put ornaments around the outside of the light fixture as desired.

Beaded Beauty Candles

Shown on page 137

What you need

- **Tape measure**
- **Beading wire**
- **3-inch pillar candle**
- **Beads in desired colors**
- **Wire cutters**
- **Short straight pins**

What you do

Measure around the pillar candle with the tape measure and add 3 inches. Cut the beading wire that length. Lay the beads out in the order that they are to be strung. String the beads and wrap around the candle. Secure in the back by twisting the wire. To make the beaded pendants (on red candle), thread the beads on a wire pin, and string onto the threaded beads in order desired. Trim any excess wire. Poke the little straight pins under the beaded wire to hold in place if necessary. *Never leave a burning candle unattended.*

Monogramed Goblets

Shown on page 138

What you need

- **Purchased stemmed goblets**
- **3-D letter stickers**
- **Ribbon to match goblet colors**

What you do

Be sure the goblets are clean and dry. Decide where to put the monogram and at what angle. Adhere the sticker letter to the base of the goblet. Tie a matching ribbon around the base of the goblet.

Snowflake Illusion

Shown on page 139

What you need

- **6x6-inch square or desired size of colored tissue paper (finished snowflake should be slightly smaller than circumference of plates)**
- **Pencil**
- **Scissors**
- **Two clear glass plates**

What you do

Trace or photocopy one of the patterns, below, if desired. Fold the square of tissue paper in half and then in half again. Fold it one more time bringing the folded edges together creating a triangle shape. Lay the pattern on the fold and mark with pencil, or cut shapes freehand. Cut on folded lines only. Open up the snowflake. Lay between the two glass plates.

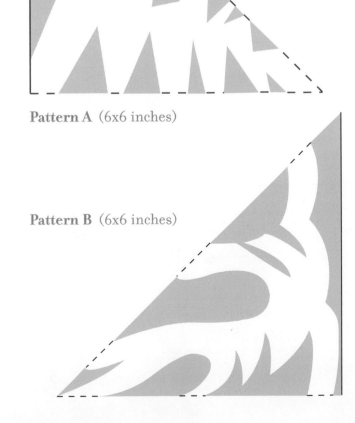

Pattern A (6x6 inches)

Pattern B (6x6 inches)

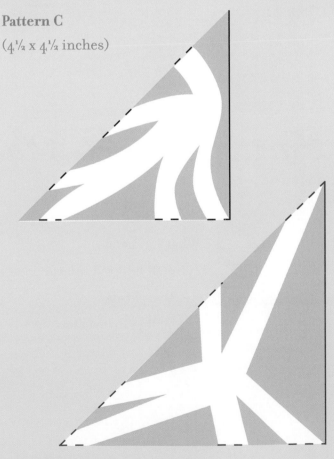

Pattern C
(4½ x 4½ inches)

Pattern D (5½ x 5½ inches)

Snowflake Patterns

the blue areas are the areas to be cut out

149

Fortune Cookie Fun

Shown on page 141

What you need

- **Purchased fortune cookies (available in bulk at Asian food stores)**
- **Candy coating pellets in green and white**
- **Microwave**
- **Coarse green sugar**
- **Wax paper**
- **Red gumdrops**

What you do

Melt the candy pellets in the microwave as directed on package. Dip one end of the fortune cookie in the candy. Sprinkle with coarse green sugar. Lay on waxed paper to dry or prop up in clean egg carton that has been lined with waxed paper.

To make the wreath, arrange on a circular plate and add red gumdrops between the fortune cookies to resemble berries.

Fairest-of-All Placecard

Shown on page 140

What you need

- **Small beveled mirror**
- **Glass paints**
- **Small paintbrushes**

What you do

Be sure the mirror is clean and dry. Decide on the design and name desired and practice painting the designs on paper first. Paint design and name on mirror. Allow to dry following manufacturer's instructions.

Heavenly Napkin Rings

Shown on page 144

What you need

- **Art from page 154**
- **Scissors**
- **Crafts glue**
- **Fine gold glitter**
- **Beads in desired colors**
- **Fine elastic beading cording**

What you do

Color copy or scan the angel art. Cut out. Run a fine line of glue around the edge and dust with glitter. Allow to dry. Cut the cording to measure about 7 inches long. Tie a knot in the end. Thread on the beads and tie a knot at the end. Add a drop of glue on the knot and let dry. Glue the art onto the beaded string. Place around the napkin.

Chocolate Lover's Placecard

Shown on page 145

What you need

- **Purchased chocolate cup (available at fine candy stores)**
- **Coarse white sugar**
- **Toothpick**
- **3x4-inch piece of white cardstock**
- **2x3½-inch piece of white cardstock**
- **Decorative scissors**
- **Dimensional stickers such as Pop Dots**
- **Gold marker**

What you do

Trim the two pieces of cardstock with decorative-edge scissors. Write the name on the littlest piece. Place the little piece on top of the bigger one spacing them apart with the pop dots and putting the toothpick in the middle. Add a piece of tape if necessary to secure. Fill the chocolate cup with the white sugar. Insert the name card in the sugar.

Use the Vintage Bird art to create
the ornaments on page 52.

Use the Joy art to create the greeting card on page 118.

Use the Santa art to create the Santa placecards on page 135.

153

Use the Angel art to create the napkin rings on page 144.

154

THE ANIMALS CHRISTMAS

Use the vintage Santa art to create the greeting card on page 119.

Messages for inside your holiday cards

May all your favorite things surround you at Christmastime.

❈

Peace, hope, and joy be yours at Christmastime and always.

❈

"God Bless us everyone!"

❈

"For unto you is born this day in the city of David, a Savior,
who is Christ the Lord."   Luke 2:11

❈

May all the sweet things of Christmas find their way to you.

❈

Bow Making

Decide what kind of bow you want to make.
Because there are so many choices when you purchase ribbon, have in mind the kind of finished bow you want. If you use wire-edge ribbon, your bow will stand up better and look crisper. Non wire-edge ribbon will work as well, but the finished bow will be limper and more flowing. Ribbon comes in all widths, patterns, and styles. If you want to make a small bow, use narrow ribbon. Even some narrow ribbon comes with a wire edge. The wider the ribbon the more yardage you will need. See the table below for approximate lengths of ribbon based on how wide the ribbon is.
Refer to numbered diagrams, opposite.

1. Lay the piece of ribbon on a flat surface.
(These measurements are assuming that you are using a ribbon that is 1½ inches wide.) Starting from the left side of the ribbon, about 12 inches in from the end, accordion fold the ribbon back and forth until there are at least four loops on each side. The 12-inch length that you left on the left side will be one of the tails. Be sure there are at least 15 inches of ribbon left on the right side when you are done making the accordion loops. That 15 inches will make the center loop and other tail.

2. Squeeze the loops together in the middle.
Starting at the center of a 24-inch piece of 24-gauge wind the wire around the center at least 2 times. Twist the wires together. You should have a length of wire coming up at the top and the bottom after you are done winding the wire in the middle.

3. Now this is the tricky (but not difficult) part.
Pull the top piece of ribbon to the left and make a loop that looks like a center of a bow right where you wound the wire. Squeeze it in and let the ribbon drape to the bottom right.

4. Take the bottom wire and wind it around the
loop where you squeezed it. Wrap the wire around at least twice. Twist it with the other wire behind the bow to secure the middle loop. Don't trim the wires—you'll need them to attach the bow to a wreath, a package, or wherever your awesome bow is to be used. Pull apart the bow loops to make them the fullness that you like.
Trim the ends of the ribbons the length you want. You can cut them straight or notch them by folding each end in half the long way and cutting a V notch.

Approximate Ribbon Yardages to Make a Bow
½-inch-wide ribbon = 4 feet (1⅓ yards)
1-inch-wide ribbon = 7 feet (2⅓ yards)
1½-inch-wide ribbon = 9 feet (3 yards)
2-inch-wide ribbon =12 feet (4 yards)
2½-inch-wide ribbon = 15 feet (5 yards)
3-inch-wide ribbon = 18 feet (6 yards)

1

2

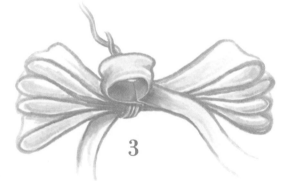

3

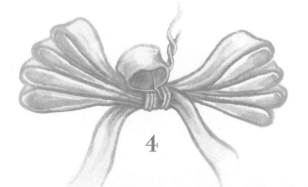

4

Sources

ArtEmboss metal
American Art Clay Co. Inc.
4717 W. 16th Street
Indianapolis, IN 46222

Cookie cutters, Decorative sugars, Dragees
Maid of Scandinavia by Sweet Celebrations
800-328-6722
www.sweetc.com

Gem adhesive
Quick Grip all-purpose permanent adhesive
Beacon Adhesives
125 MacQuesten Parkway South, Mount
Vernon, NY 10550
914-699-3400
www.beaconcreates.com

Knitted Projects
Coats
P.O. Box 1530
Albany, GA 31703
800-445-1173
www.modadea.com

Scrapbooking decorative paper clips
Nostalgiques /The Attic Collection
EK Success, P.O. Box 1141
Clifton, NJ 07014-1141
800-524-1349
www.eksuccess.com

Index

Acknowledgements

Lyne Neymeyer (book design)
Lyne has designed dozens of best-selling books for leading publishers across the country. Lyne's talents are many—she is an accomplished photographer, teaches book design at the university level, and has a knack for finding rare and vintage books. Lyne brings a wealth of talent to the book-making process.

Pete Krumhardt (photographer)
Known across the country for his amazing images, Pete is best known for his use and understanding of light and his work photographing gardens and nature. His images can be seen in various publications across the country including Better Homes and Gardens® publications.

Dean Tanner (photographer)
Dean's beautiful food photography can be seen in major publications and advertising across the country including Cuisine® magazine. His great eye for composition and color make him an outstanding photographer for every subject.

Jennifer Peterson (food artist)
Jennifer's amazing talents include creating art from food as she designs and decorates cookies and cakes. Also an accomplished food stylist, Jennifer's work appears in many publications across the country including Better Homes and Gardens books and Cuisine magazine.

About the Author:

Carol Field Dahlstrom has produced over 75 crafts, food, decorating, children's, and holiday books for Better Homes and Gardens®, Bookspan®, and from her own publishing company, Brave Ink Press. She has made numerous television, radio, and speaking appearances sharing her books and encouraging simple and productive ways to spend family time together. Her creative vision and experience make her books fun as well as informative. She lives with her family in the country near Des Moines, Iowa, where she writes and designs from her studio.

Also from Brave Ink Press

If you liked this book, look for other books from Brave Ink Press:

- **Simply Christmas**
- **Christmas—Make it Sparkle**
- **Beautiful Christmas**
- **An Ornament a Day**
- **College Kids Cook**
- **Cool Crafts to Make even if you don't have a Creative Bone in your body!**

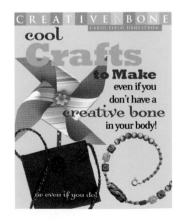

To order books visit us at www.braveink.com

Brave Ink Press—the **"I can do that!"** books™

160